MIKHAIL GORBACHEV

MIKHAIL GORBACHEV

BY MICHAEL KORT

FRANKLIN WATTS
NEW YORK LONDON TORONTO SYDNEY
AN IMPACT BIOGRAPHY 1990

HOUSTON PUBLIC LIBRARY

Map by Joe LeMonnier

Photographs courtesy of: Novosti from Sovfoto: pp. 42, 68 top;
Tass from Sovfoto: pp. 68 bottom, 81, 92 bottom, 96, 104,
111, 124; Reuters/Bettmann Newsphotos: pp. 49, 93 bottom, 99,
116, 121, 135, 150; UPI/Bettmann Newsphotos: pp. 92 top,
93 top; Wide World Photos: pp. 140, 143.

Library of Congress Cataloging-in-Publication Data

Kort, Michael, 1944–
Mikhail Gorbachev / by Michael Kort.
p.   cm.—(An Impact biography)
Summary: Discusses the life of Mikhail Gorbachev
from his formative years to the present, and examines
the reform he has introduced to the Soviet Union.
Includes bibliographical references and index.
ISBN 0-531-10941-0
1. Gorbachev, Mikhail Sergeevich, 1931–   —Juvenile literature.
2. Heads of state—Soviet Union—Biography—Juvenile literature.
3. Soviet Union—Politics and government—1985–   —Juvenile
literatures. [1. Gorbachev, Mikhail Sergeevich, 1931–   . 2. Heads of
state. 3. Soviet Union—Politics and government—1985–   ] I. Title.
DK290.3.G67K67   1990
947.085′4′092—dc20
[B]
90-37078   CIP   AC

For Carol

CONTENTS

INTRODUCTION

In December of 1989, as the 1980s drew to a close, a major American news organization hailed the Soviet Union's Mikhail Gorbachev as "Man of the Decade." The honor was richly deserved. Since 1985, when Gorbachev first came to power, the world had witnessed dramatic changes. A process of unprecedented reform had begun in the Soviet Union that held the promise of transforming a harsh, stagnant, inefficient one-party dictatorship into a dynamic and relatively open society. The Cold War, a forty-five-year era marked by endless tension and a fantastically expensive arms race between the Soviet Union and the United States, was rapidly coming to an end. In Eastern Europe, corrupt and inept communist governments installed by the Soviet Union after World War II were collapsing, swept away by a huge upsurge of popular will and democratic feeling. While no individual could possibly have caused all this alone, there was no doubt that one man—Mikhail Sergeyevich Gorbachev—had done far more than anyone else to bring these changes about. Without him, they might well not have happened at all, certainly not as soon or as quickly.

While Gorbachev is not a "miracle" as one leading American observer of the Soviet Union called him, he is a remarkable historical figure. In a very short time he has established himself as the finest leader his country has known in generations. He is also widely recognized as the most respected political leader in the world of his own generation. Millions of people in dozens of countries looked to Gorbachev because they saw him as an international statesman in a class by himself, a visionary working for a better future not just for his own country, but for all nations. By 1990 Mikhail Gorbachev already had earned an honored place in history. Even if he does no more, his life will have had an impact upon our world.

1
A YOUTH FROM THE PROVINCES

Mikhail Gorbachev is a man seemingly destined to beat the odds. He was born in a small village in 1931, when a government campaign to end private farming brought terror and death to the countryside of the Soviet Union. When hundreds of thousands of Soviet officials and millions of ordinary citizens were imprisoned and murdered during an even greater wave of terror during the 1930s, Mikhail's immediate family emerged relatively unscathed. The German invasion of the Soviet Union and the horrors of World War II (which claimed at least 20 million Soviet lives between 1941 and 1945) again spared Mikhail, his parents, and his grandparents.

Upon graduating from secondary school in 1950, nineteen-year-old Mikhail defied odds of 25 to 1 to gain admission to Moscow State University, the country's leading institution of higher learning. As an adult Gorbachev overcame even greater odds. He rose through the ranks of political office to become general secretary of the Communist Party and president of the Soviet Union, the undisputed leader of his country. Since coming to power in 1985, Gorbachev has gambled his political future on an attempt to introduce drastic reforms in many areas of Soviet life. He has yet to beat the enormous odds against trying to change so much so fast in the Soviet Union.

The Union of Soviet Socialist Republics, the formal

11

name for the country Gorbachev leads, is the giant among the nations of the world. It covers 8.5 million square miles (22 million sq km), one-seventh of the world's entire land surface. It is more than twice as large as Canada and almost three times as large as the United States excluding Alaska. The Soviet Union's western borders are in Central Europe; its eastern border, the Pacific coast, is 6,000 miles (about 8,700 km) and the full length of Asia away. Its northernmost reaches are icy rocks in waters well above the Arctic Circle, while its southern tip is baking sand bordering on the deserts of central Asia.

This vast expanse contains many diverse wonders of nature. Frigid tundra grasses extend for thousands of miles in the far north. The rest of the north and much of the center of the country are covered by the largest forest in the world, called the taiga. South of the taiga a great prairie called the steppe contains some of the most fertile soil in the world. The Soviet Union is also a land of soaring, snow-covered mountains and flat, burning deserts. It has deep, clear, freshwater lakes and shallow saltwater seas, rushing rivers and stagnant marshlands, barren arctic islands and lush subtropical peninsulas. It is blessed with an unmatched treasure trove of natural resources, including some of the world's largest deposits of iron, coal, oil, and gold.

The Soviet population is as varied as its geography. Barely half the people are Russian, or Great Russian, as they are sometimes called. The Great Russians compose the dominant nationality in the Soviet Union, and are the group to which Gorbachev belongs. The rest of the population, conquered or annexed over centuries of Russian expansion, makes the Soviet Union one of the most ethnically diverse nations in the world. Two groups, the Ukrainians and the Belorussians, are closely related to the Great Russians. Although each group has its own historical identity, they speak languages that are similar to, but distinct from, Russian. The Soviet Union is also

12

the home of the Latvians, Lithuanians, Estonians, Germans, Uzbeks, Kazakhs, Jews, Armenians, and many others—over 100 distinct ethnic groups in all. Its total population is over 280 million, making the Soviet Union the world's third most populous nation, after China and India.

Despite its problems, the Soviet Union today is, along with the United States, one of the world's two military superpowers. It is the world's third greatest economic power, trailing the United States and Japan as a producer of goods and services. Its influence is worldwide.

This was not always the case. Before 1917, the Soviet Union was known as the Russian Empire. It was a huge and formidable state, then as now the largest country in the world. But economically, the Russian Empire lagged behind the modern states of western Europe and North America. Its emperor, or *tsar,* held enormous power, far more than any of the few remaining European monarchs of the time. In March 1917, in the middle of World War I, Tsar Nicholas II was overthrown. That revolution brought to power certain people who dreamed of turning Russia into a democratic state with a modern free enterprise economy modeled after those of the advanced countries of Europe and the Americas.

That dream did not last. Only eight months later, on the night of November 7–8, 1917, a second revolution brought a new group to power. They were called the Bolsheviks, led by an extraordinarily able and ruthless politician named Vladimir Lenin. Lenin and the Bolsheviks were followers of Karl Marx, a German thinker who advocated the overthrow of capitalism and its replacement by socialism. The Bolsheviks' goal was to turn Russia into a socialist society in which all private property would be abolished. The state would own all the factories, farms, and natural resources. Instead of competing with one another as they did under capitalism, people would work together, cooperatively, for the gen-

NORWAY

SWEDEN

FINLAND

BARENTS SEA

KARA SEA

ESTONIAN
S.S.R.
BALTIC SEA
Tallinn
LATVIAN S.S.R.

LITHUANIAN
S.S.R.   Riga
Vilnius   Lake
Lagodu
Leningrad

POLAND

Minsk

BELORUSSIAN
S.S.R.

Moscow ●

Gorki ○

URAL MTS.

RUSSIAN   SOVIET

MOLD-
AVIAN   ● Kiev
S.S.R.   UKRAINIAN
S.S.R. ○ Khurkov
● Kishinev

Odessa

*BLACK
SEA*

Volgograd ○

CAUCASIAS
MOUNTAINS

GEORGIAN
S.S.R.

*CASPIAN
SEA*

KAZAKH S.S.R.

TURKEY   Tbilisi
Yerevan
ARMENIAN
S.S.R.

*ARAL
SEA*

Baku

AZERBAIJAN
S.S.R.

TURKMEN
S.S.R.   UZBEK
S.S.R.   Tashkent   ● Alma-Ata

Frunze

IRAQ

Ashkhabad

KIRGIZ S.S.R.

IRAN

Dushanbe   TADZHIK S.S.R.

BERING SEA

SIBERIAN SEA

LAPTEV SEA

S I B E R I A

SEA OF OKHOTSK

FEDERATED SOCIALIST REPUBLIC

vosibirsk

Lake Baikal

Vladivostok

SEA OF JAPAN

MONGOLIA

N. KOREA

CHINA

S. KOREA

Union of Soviet Socialist Republics

- ● Capital cities
- ○ Major cities

0   600 Miles

eral good. Rather than have individuals make their own often selfish decisions about the economy, all economic activity would be planned by the state.

To accomplish this, Lenin and the Bolsheviks believed that their party alone had to make all the decisions. They therefore began to suppress all other political groups—whether these believed in restoring the tsar, in converting Russia into a democratic state with a free enterprise economy, or even in turning Russia into a socialist society, but one in which the Bolsheviks shared power with other groups. The result was a ferocious civil war that lasted from 1918 to 1921. It is likely that one of the participants in that struggle was Gorbachev's grandfather Andrei. Although Andrei Gorbachev was a prosperous peasant he was an early supporter of the new Bolshevik government. By the early 1920s he was an active member of Lenin's party. The war ended with a Bolshevik victory and the establishment of a one-party dictatorship with Lenin as its head. All political opposition was swiftly and brutally eliminated. Under Lenin, who led the country until his death in 1924, Russia's name was changed to the Union of Soviet Socialist Republics (USSR) and the Bolshevik party was renamed the Communist Party of the Soviet Union.

After Lenin's death there was a struggle for power among his lieutenants. By 1929, Joseph Stalin had won that struggle and consolidated his power. Thereafter, Stalin continued to build his strength by periodically demoting people, or driving them out of the party entirely, and replacing them with new recruits totally dependent on him and his growing political machine. An important part of that machine was the secret police, which Stalin used against ordinary citizens and members of the party alike. By the end of the 1920s, one of Stalin's supporters at the local level who loyally carried out orders from Moscow was Andrei Gorbachev.

Andrei Gorbachev and his family lived in a village near

16

the town of Stavropol. Stavropol is in the North Caucasus, a region that did not become part of Russia until the second half of the eighteenth century. It lies between Russia's two famous rivers, the storied Don to the west and the mighty Volga to the east. To the south loom the magnificent Caucasus Mountains, rising thousands of feet above the steppe and stretching east to west from the Black Sea to the Caspian. The plain below has the rich black earth of the Russian steppe that in the North Caucasus is often over 6 feet (1.8 meters) deep. The excellent soil and relatively favorable climate of the North Caucasus have made the region one of the Soviet Union's most important agricultural areas.

The city of Stavropol was founded in 1777 as a fortress to defend against Moslem tribesmen to the south, whom the Russians fought for a century before finally conquering them. That fierce struggle has been immortalized by Russia's greatest writers, including Mikhail Lermontov in *A Hero of Our Times,* Alexander Pushkin in *The Captive of the Caucasus,* and Leo Tolstoy in *Hadji Murad.* The first Russians in the area were peasants fleeing a slavelike condition in the western and central parts of their country known as serfdom. Serfdom existed in Russia from the sixteenth century until it was abolished in 1861. In the North Caucasus and other frontier areas far from the center of power in Moscow, these runaways managed to avoid serfdom and develop a free and self-reliant lifestyle that was exceptional in the oppressive Russian Empire. After serfdom was abolished more migrants from central Russia arrived and Russians gradually became the majority of the population in the North Caucasus.

Mikhail Gorbachev was born to Sergei and Maria Panteleyvna Gorbachev in a village close to Stavropol called Privolnoye, which in Russian means "free" or "spacious." Today the Stavropol region of about 30,000 square miles (77,720 sq km) is home to about three million people, including Gorbachev's mother, now in her seventies. She has not let her son's success move her out of her small brick cottage or away from her vegetable garden, chickens, and cow. Maria Panteleyvna obviously prefers her familiar surroundings where much remains as it was in her younger days. In Privolnoye many residents continue the old custom of freshly painting their houses blue and white each year and planting flowers in their gardens in time for Easter. Young boys still swim in a nearby river, as they did when Mikhail was a boy. Maria Panteleyvna could count on visits from her son, whose rise through the ranks never made him too important to return to Privolnoye regularly to see his mother and visit the gravesite of his father, who died in 1976.

Even in fertile areas such as Stavropol, life for the Russian peasants has never been easy. They must struggle against a short growing season and an inequitable supply of rainfall. The most plentiful rains fall on the poor, thin soil of the forest zone, while the more fertile black earth regions often do not get enough. On top of nature's hardships, the Russian peasants endured oppression from their government. Even after serfdom was abolished, the government for over forty years regulated many aspects of peasant life, all the while taxing the peasants to the limit. Only during the last ten years of the tsarist regime did the government make a serious attempt to improve the peasantry's ability to make a living.

The Bolshevik Revolution did not make life easier in the Russian countryside. During the civil war that followed, both the Bolsheviks and their opponents took what they needed from the peasants by force. By 1921, famine, an old nemesis, again stalked the land. During the next eight years the government, this time under the victorious Communist party, generally left the peasants alone. This short period was the golden age for the Russian peasant. The landlords had been driven away by the Bolshevik Revolution, and most of their land had been turned over to the peasants. The peasants prospered as never before, masters of the land they had always craved and free to grow and sell what they could.

Then came Stalin's consolidation of power. Ever since they had seized power, the Communists wanted to modernize their country's lagging economy. The Communists believed that socialism could only be realized in an advanced industrial society. But in 1917 most of Russia was still a backward agricultural society, unable to produce the machines and goods required for modern industry. Little was done during the 1920s; recovering from World War I and the civil war was difficult enough.

By 1929, however, the recovery was complete. Power was in the hands of a group led by Stalin who were determined to industrialize the country in ten years. In order to do this, the party leadership decreed that development would proceed according to a five-year plan to make the most of all available resources. Most of those resources were then diverted to investments in basic heavy industry like steel, machine tools, fuels, and armaments. Very little was left over for housing and consumer goods. This led to a great deal of suffering, and to the greatest peacetime decline in a country's standard of living ever recorded.

Among the most important of those resources was food. The problem, according to Stalin, was that the Soviet peasantry working on its small farms could not produce enough food to feed growing numbers of factory workers in the cities and to export in exchange for necessary machinery. Also, millions of peasants working their own farms, buying and selling as they pleased in private markets, were viewed as so many small capitalists. This was unacceptable in Stalin's vision of a socialist society.

19

The program to overcome this was called collectivization. Its intent was to combine the small private peasant farms into large cooperative farms worked by many families. The expectation was that with larger fields, modern equipment, and cooperative work, production would increase and provide greater resources for the drive towards industrialization. Also, the government could control 200,000 large collective farms better than 20 million scattered peasant homesteads.

But there was one unavoidable problem: the peasantry overwhelmingly wanted to keep their small farms. This did not stop Stalin and the Communist party. Late in 1929 they attacked with abrupt frightening force. The full power of the state, spearheaded by heavily armed units of the secret police, struck the countryside. A terrible slaughter resulted. Anyone who resisted was killed; entire villages were machine-gunned into submission. The following eyewitness account provides only a glimpse of the horrible panorama that was the Soviet countryside during the late 1920s and early 1930s:

> *For three days . . . a bloody battle was waged between the . . . people and the authorities. . . . This revolt was cruelly punished. Thousands of peasants, workers, soldiers, and officers paid for the attempt with their lives, while the survivors were deported to concentration camps. . . . mass executions were carried out near the* balkis *(ravines). The soil of this region was soaked in blood. After the executions, these villages were set on fire.*[1]

Those peasants who were not forced onto the collective farms suffered an even worse fate. They usually were the more prosperous peasants, or *kulaks*. Along with their wives and children, the *kulaks* were either killed or deported to remote areas or to a growing network of slave-labor camps. Often entire families committed suicide. Those who did not endured a living death:

> *Trainloads of deported peasants left for the icy North, the forests, the steppes, the deserts. These were whole populations, denuded of everything; the old folk starved to death in mid-journey, newborn babies were buried on the banks of the roadside, and each wilderness had its crop of little crosses of boughs of white wood.*[2]

Nobody knows the exact toll collectivization had on human life. According to Stalin, who was not likely to underestimate, ten million peasants died. And that was not the end of it. By 1931 the government had largely won its battle with the people; the majority of peasants were on collective farms. But the turmoil and destruction of the battle led to a poor harvest in 1932. This did not deter the state from taking even more grain for its own use than it had the year before. The result was a famine centered in the Ukraine and the North Caucasus. At least five million more peasants died in what, in reality, was a famine engineered by the government to break resistance to collectivization.

The death toll reached one million in the North Caucasus, where the old traditions of freedom seem to have led to especially strong resistance to collectivization. In the fall of 1932 Stalin sent a special commission to the North Caucasus. The commission was headed by Lazar Kaganovich, Stalin's most ruthless troubleshooter, and included Henrik Yadoga, the head of the secret police. One of its junior members was a young man named Mikhail Suslov. He would endure to become the second most powerful man in the Soviet Union in the 1970s under Leonid Brezhnev. As such he was responsible for advancing the careers of many ambitious party loyalists. One of them would be Mikhail Gorbachev.

Years later when General Secretary Mikhail Gorbachev discussed collectivization, he admitted that mistakes had been made and that what he called "blunders" and "excesses" had occurred. But he would not repudiate what Stalin and the party did. Collectivization, he insisted, whatever its shortcomings, remained a "great historic act."[3] If this assessment seems surprising coming from a man whose policies seem to be reversing collectivization to some degree, it may be because Gorbachev is recalling the active role his grandfather played in collectivization. Andrei Gorbachev must have thrown his full effort into the campaign, since he emerged as the first chairman of the local collective farm.

Regardless of what Gorbachev might say, collectivization was a disaster. Many peasants killed their livestock rather than give them up to the collective. More than half the country's horses, nearly half its cows, and about two-thirds of its sheep did not survive collectivization.

Another casualty was the will to farm. By the mid-1930s, two types of Soviet farms had replaced the old peasant farms. The collective farms, or *kolkhozes,* were technically owned and managed by their members. In reality, they were run by officials appointed by the Communist party. The collectives had to deliver what they produced to the state. They received very low prices for their goods, often less than it cost to produce them. Each member was then paid a percentage of what the farm received, depending on the work performed. The problem is that there was so little to go around that even the hardest workers received very little. What this meant is that collective farm members had little incentive to work. The result, from the 1930s to the present, has been inefficient farming methods, low productivity, and a country unable to feed itself properly.

The peasants survived only because they were allowed to keep small private plots. Here a family could raise what it needed and sell whatever was left over on the open market. These tiny plots together amounted to only 3 to 4 percent of the country's farmland, but produced about 25 percent of its food.

The second type of new Soviet farm was the *sovkhoz,* or state farm. Here the peasants were employees who received a straight wage. But the wages were low, the living conditions terrible, and the morale as bad and willingness to work as low as on the collectives. Like the collective farmers, the state farm workers have depended on their private plots to survive. Since the 1950s, the Soviet government has invested enormous funds in the huge state farms. But as on the collectives, it has never allowed the state farm workers themselves to make any important decisions. As a result, the state farms have become only a growing part of the Soviet Union's agricultural problem, not a solution to it.

It was during the very peak of collectivization, on March 2, 1931, that Mikhail Sergeyevich Gorbachev was born. (Old friends say he took after his mother, Maria, the "energetic one," rather than his father, Sergei, who is remembered as the "quiet one.") Mikhail's grandfather Andrei was the chairman of the local collective farm, which means that he was a trusted party loyalist. His father was a driver of a combine-harvester, a job with much higher status than that of an ordinary farmer. Those who worked the large farm machines, in fact, were not assigned to collective farms. They were attached to what were called Machine Tractor Stations. The MTS's supplied large machines to many collective farms in return for part of the harvest, and were one of the tools the state used to control those collectives.

In effect, young Mikhail at birth became part of the new governing elite of the countryside. That was virtually a necessity for a new baby in the North Caucasus in those days, as the tragic effects of collectivization and famine raged across the land. In some villages *none* of the infants under the age of two survived. An eyewitness recorded the following scene: "Houses with boarded-up windows, empty barnyards, abandoned equipment in fields. And terrifying mortality, especially among the children. . . ."[4]

There was no security once collectivization was completed. One of Stalin's techniques to gain absolute power was to periodically demote and arrest huge numbers of party members. This presumably would assure that no group could form against him and that all orders were carried out. In these campaigns the victims would be accused of all kinds of crimes they could not have possibly committed, but which the state propaganda network convinced millions of Soviet citizens were actually taking place.

The campaigns, called purges, hit their destructive peak between 1936 and 1938. Millions of people, both party loyalists and ordinary citizens, were arrested. Many were shot outright, but most were sent to what was the largest network of slave-labor camps in history, the notorious Soviet *Gulag,* where uncounted millions died. The endless drumbeat of propaganda, which stressed how the country was infested with "counterrevolutionaries," "wreckers," and agents of foreign capitalist powers, drove the country to a fever pitch of hysteria and fear.

In the North Caucasus, as in many other regions, entire local party organizations were arrested. Among the victims was the head of the entire regional organization, the man who had been in charge of pushing collectivization to its successful conclusion. The purge apparently struck Mikhail's extended family, when his maternal grandfather reportedly was arrested. However, he was fortunate enough to be released after a year and a half. Despite this particular outcome, collectivization and the purges almost certainly claimed the lives of some people Mikhail knew, and he must have been deeply affected by the atmosphere of fear that pervaded the country. As a schoolboy attending a primary school in Privolnoye, he must have heard stories of destroyed houses, arrests, shootings, and deportations that must have been shocking and frightening to young, impressionable ears. But in the late 1930s, the brunt of the storm passed over Mikhail. Unlike millions of his peers, he did not have one or both parents torn from him. He never had to go to a prison or transfer point to inquire desperately about the fate of those who in normal times would be taking care of him. Nor did he have to wait for years, struggling against all reason to keep hope alive, trying to fight the system and prove that in the case of *his* father or mother, a terrible injustice had been done.

Stalin ended his great purge in 1938. The country then experienced a few years of relative peace. But it was not for long. In 1939, World War II broke out. The Soviet Union stayed out of the war for two years because of the infamous Nazi-Soviet treaty of August 1939. This was Stalin's pact with the German dictator Adolf Hitler, under which the Soviet Union and Germany publicly pledged not to attack each other and secretly divided Eastern Europe between themselves. The Soviets, while officially neutral in the war, continued to trade and maintain friendly relations with the Germans, leaving Hitler free to wage war on Western Europe. In June of 1941, the Soviet Union's short-lived peace came to an end when Germany invaded its former ally. The Soviet Union was shockingly unprepared for war. The Germans drove deep into Soviet territory. Sergei Gorbachev, along with virtually all able-bodied men, was drafted into the Soviet army.

The first two years of the war were disastrous for the Soviet Union. The Germans crushed most of the Soviet forces in their path and took huge numbers of prisoners. The Nazis also were brutal to Soviet civilians. Although all Soviet citizens were treated cruelly and often murdered, the worse suffering befell Soviet Jews, whom the

Nazis had decided to systematically and totally wipe out. The Soviets did manage to save their two main cities, Moscow and Leningrad, in heroic stands, but large parts of the Soviet Union were occupied and brutalized by the Germans, some regions for as long as two years.

The Stavropol region fell to the Nazis in the summer of 1942. The Germans stayed for five months. It is unlikely they bothered to occupy Privolnoye, a small village far from a railway line or even a major road. Soviet records show that the Germans murdered 10,000 people during their brief occupation. But horrible as that figure may be, in reality the German occupation of the Stavropol region was less harsh than in many other places. This is because the Germans decided to appeal to the resentment many of the non-Russian people of the region felt for their rulers in Moscow. The Germans also allowed local farmers to disband the hated collective farms. Churches, closed by the officially atheist Communist government, were permitted to reopen. And the curriculum in the schools, which children, including Mikhail Gorbachev, continued to attend, reflected the Nazi rather than the Communist version of the truth.

Unlike many other parts of the Soviet Union, the Stavropol region had very few anti-German partisan groups able to operate. The Nazis found a fairly large number of civilians to cooperate with them, including some members of the local Moslem ethnic minority groups. A terrible fate awaited those people once the Germans were driven out, however. Stalin decided to blame entire peoples for what a few among them had done. So, when Soviet forces reoccupied these regions, they deported entire ethnic groups to remote eastern parts of the country. This created a new set of ethnic grievances within the Soviet Union. Some were redressed in the 1950s and 1960s, but others have remained for General Secretary and President Gorbachev to resolve.

Gorbachev spent the war, including the months of

German occupation, in Privolnoye. For three months he did not attend school, possibly because of the disruption caused by the Soviet retreat and German occupation of the region. His mother has provided another reason for her son's truancy: he lacked the necessary shoes and clothing. An urgent letter from Sergei insisting that his son attend school then led Maria Gorbachev to sell some farm animals to raise the money to buy Mikhail what he needed. He was readmitted to school after his mother convinced the principal that her son would make up the large amount of work he had missed. Mikhail also spent part of the war years living with his father's parents. He was especially close to his grandmother. In spite of the Soviet regime's official establishment of atheism, Gorbachev's grandmother remained a devout member of the Russian Orthodox Church. When Mikhail was born, she insisted he be baptized; while he lived with her during the war, she regularly took him to church.*

Like most ordinary Soviet civilians, Mikhail suffered hardships during the war. With the men away at the front, women and children had to work the farms. Children as young as twelve sometimes worked eleven or more hours per day to feed the country. Mikhail also learned about the high price of combat; a local war memorial contains the names of seven Gorbachevs. They were among the 20 million Soviet citizens killed between 1941 and 1945. (By comparison, the United States lost 400,000 in the war.)

Still, Mikhail, his mother, and his grandparents endured. During the fighting, Privolnoye's distance from the railroads and main roads meant that the armies passed it by. The Germans retreated from the Stavropol region

---

*Those who do not believe in God are called atheists. Karl Marx was an atheist who also believed that religion was a device rulers used to keep the majority of the people under control. His followers therefore have always been hostile to all religions. In the Soviet Union, the practice of religion has not only been discouraged, but has often resulted in persecution.

in January of 1943. At the end of the war came perhaps the greatest gift of all. Sergei, although wounded, had survived. He returned home from the war decorated with his share of medals.

In May 1945 Germany was finally defeated. With the defeat of Japan in September, World War II came to an end. Although the Soviet Union was on the winning side, four years of fighting a merciless enemy had devastated the western part of the country. Approximately 70,000 villages, 100,000 collective farms, 40,000 miles of railway line, and over half of all urban housing in European Russia were completely or partially destroyed. Many of the Soviet Union's most important industrial areas lay in ruins. Millions lived in holes in the ground. Observers have left graphic impressions of the scene, among them Gorbachev himself, who saw some of the destruction several years after the war ended:

> *I saw with my own eyes the ruined Stalingrad, Rostov, Orel, Kursk, and Voronezh. And how many ruined cities there were: Leningrad, Kiev, Minsk, Odessa, Sevastopol, Smolensk, Brinask, Novgorod. . . . Everything lay in ruins: hundreds and thousands of cities, towns and villages, factories and mills. Our most valuable monuments of culture were plundered or destroyed—picture galleries, palaces, libraries and cathedrals.*[5]

The immediate postwar years were very difficult. Food was scarce—the 1946 harvest was disastrously small—and some parts of the country experienced famine when the government insisted on taking as much grain as usual from the farmers. Stalin's regime also insisted that all available resources be directed to rebuilding basic heavy industries. This left virtually nothing for housing or consumer goods, and meant that the Soviet standard of living remained miserably low.

For Gorbachev life was not easy, but as the son of a family with strong party credentials it was better than for most. He was able to return to school, though not under easy conditions. Every day he had to walk 12 miles each way to his high school, often in bitter, freezing weather. This burden soon became too heavy even for a determined and ambitious youth like Mikhail Gorbachev. Sergei therefore rented his son space in a room near the school with two other boys. It cost 150 rubles a year, a large sum for an ordinary Soviet wage earner, especially considering that the room was not heated during the winter. Young Mikhail made his family's sacrifice count by working hard at his studies. His teachers liked the cooperative boy from Privolnoye who enjoyed music and playacting and made a point of staying out of trouble. The school's principal remembered the enthusiasm of her most famous student, how he answered the most difficult questions and "also gave the most elaborate answers, our Misha Mikhail Sergeyevich Gorbachev."[6] Upon graduation, he earned a silver medal, his school's second highest academic honor.

During those years Mikhail also had to work to help support the family—which grew by one in 1947 with the birth of a brother named Alexander *—full time during the summer and part time during the rest of the year. Mikhail worked as an assistant combine operator with his father. It was a good job, a step above the usual menial work teenagers usually could find during the summer. It was also a demanding job. In the summer it meant days baking in the scorching fields that ended with Mikhail literally caked in dust. In the winter, when he sometimes drove the combine, he had to wrap himself in straw for protection from the freezing cold and wind. Gorbachev obviously did his job well. In 1949 the har-

* Because of their sixteen-year age difference, it is unlikely that the Gorbachev brothers are close. Today Alexander is an official in the Soviet defense ministry.

vest in Privolnoye was excellent, exceeding the government's goal for the region. A number of local people were given awards for this important achievement. Among them was young Gorbachev, who received the Order of the Red Banner, a prestigious award, and especially so for someone so young. It was an important credential for any young person who wanted to make his way up the Soviet success ladder.

Aside from returning to school and working to pay his keep, Gorbachev took another major step toward building his future in Soviet society. In 1945 he joined the Communist Youth League, or "Komsomol." Membership in the Komsomol was an essential qualification for any young Soviet citizen who hoped to gain access to most career opportunities. Among other things, it was a prerequisite to membership in the Communist party. After joining it at the age of fourteen, Gorbachev worked hard, gave a great deal of his time, and established himself as an articulate and enthusiastic supporter of party goals. All this was very important in impressing the higher-ups in the Soviet bureaucratic system upon whom success and advancement depend.

Gorbachev's graduation from secondary school the next year brought him to a critical crossroads. He had to decide how and where to further his education. Gorbachev could have been satisfied with going to a university in the provinces. This was a safe route, but one that probably would have limited his future in a country where all power is concentrated at the center. Mikhail instead demonstrated some of the confidence and boldness that has since become his trademark worldwide. He applied to Moscow State University, the country's leading institution of higher learning.

With twenty-five applicants for every place, the odds obviously were against Gorbachev. But he did have some things in his favor. Aside from being a good student, Gorbachev was an outstanding Komsomol member who came from a good party family. Perhaps even more important, he was a holder of the Order of the Red Banner, a rare honor for a youth his age. In addition, Soviet authorities reserved some spaces at the prestigious university for outstanding youths from the provinces with solid working-class backgrounds.

So Mikhail Gorbachev was admitted to Moscow State University. The first of many doors he would have to pass through on his way to the top had been opened to him. The time had come to march through it and take the long road to Moscow.

2
THE FIRST
MOSCOW YEARS

While Gorbachev undoubtedly was excited about going to Moscow, the city in 1950 was an inhospitable place. For many Soviet citizens it was downright dangerous. The problem had nothing to do with the physical damage the city suffered from the war, although that certainly added to the drabness and poor living conditions of the city. The problem was Joseph Stalin.

Stalin had always been a suspicious and vicious man. The catastrophic purges of the 1930s were one example, if by far the worst, of the shattering impact his paranoia had on Soviet life. During World War II Stalin and his closest associates had to ease the pressures on the country, in order to win popular support for the life-and-death struggle against Nazi Germany. For example, restrictions on religious life were loosened and peasants received greater economic incentives to produce more. But as soon as the war was over, Stalin increased the pressure. A morbid cloud of fear again enveloped the country, particularly its capital, Moscow.

The signal for the new repression came in 1946. During the war, contacts had increased with the Western allies and many Soviet citizens had a chance to meet and even work with foreigners on an unprecedented scale. In 1946 Stalin authorized a ferocious and deadly campaign against Western influences, which he felt were a threat to his dictatorship and the Soviet order. This campaign led to thousands of arrests. Its victims often had done nothing other than read foreign books or become acquainted with someone from the West. Because Stalin translated his personal anti-Semitism into Soviet policy, a disproportionate number of victims of this campaign were Jews. They included many cultural and artistic leaders of the Jewish community. The campaign intensified after 1948, following the mysterious death of Andrei Zhdanov, one of Stalin's top lieutenants. His death was followed by the so-called Leningrad Affair, in which thousands of his associates and supporters were rounded up and arrested.

By the time Gorbachev arrived in Moscow in the fall of 1950, the political situation was deteriorating. Relations between the Soviet Union and the Western democracies led by the United States were extremely tense. Tensions had been building since 1945, ever since the Soviet Union had established its control over Poland and the other nations of Eastern Europe. Events during the late 1940s—the Berlin Airlift of 1948–9; the formation of NATO, the Western defensive military alliance, in 1949; the Soviet development and testing of an atomic bomb that same year; and the victory of the Chinese Communists in that country's civil war in the fall of 1949—intensified those tensions. The new decade began with the outbreak of the Korean War in the spring of 1950. Although that war did not pit Soviet against American troops, it did involve the United States in a shooting war with two Soviet allies, the Communist regimes in North Korea and China, thus raising tensions even more.

From the Soviet point of view, the ultimate villain was the United States. Endless anti-American propaganda instilled a fear and hatred that must have heavily influenced Soviet youths. It was difficult for many of them to overcome those feelings later in life. It is a tribute to Gorbachev that he seems to have done this.

Meanwhile, Stalin himself was declining physically and mentally, and becoming more paranoid as a result. He hatched a number of imaginary plots while Gorbachev was a student in Moscow. The most notorious of them involved the so-called Doctor's Plot of 1952–3. This "plot" involved an alleged attempt by several doctors, most of them Jewish, to kill Soviet leaders. There was, of course, no such plot; it was a tool Stalin planned to use against those whom he wanted to destroy. It seems to have been designed to serve Stalin in two ways. He was planning a massive campaign to arrest and deport most Soviet Jews to a remote region in eastern Siberia. At the same time, Stalin probably was planning to use the atmosphere of hysteria he was creating to purge the party once again. Among his intended victims were many of his closest lieutenants. They included Georgi Malenkov, the man apparently in line to succeed Stalin; Lavrenti Beria, head of the secret police; and Nikita Khrushchev, the man who actually would win the struggle for power after Stalin's death.

As his latest bizarre scheme was unfolding, Stalin suffered a massive stroke and died on March 5, 1953. His death opened a new chapter in Soviet history that was at once hopeful and dangerous. The men close to Stalin had to figure out how to lead the country without the all-powerful dictator. They knew that the miserable condition of the population had to be improved and the atmosphere of fear that dominated the country had to be lifted. This meant reforms, although there was little agreement on how many or how extensive such reforms should be. It also meant a struggle for power among men who knew nothing but a system with a dictator at the top. It was thus to a Moscow full of opportunities as well as tensions that the farm boy Mikhail Gorbachev arrived with his few belongings after his twenty-four-hour-long train ride from Stavropol.

In some ways Gorbachev was a typical new student

in Moscow. He lived in a gigantic dormitory in the center of Moscow that once had been a military barracks built by Tsar Peter the Great. In 1950 the crowded complex held over 10,000 students, with six to sixteen people crammed into each room. Mikhail and his fifteen roommates did not have a single closet in their room. Other than their beds, the only furniture was a huge table that served as a place to have breakfast, hold a meeting, or relax. The dorm was coed, although the men and women lived in separate rooms. Each floor had cooking facilities and a toilet, but no shower or bath. Bathing required a trip to one of Moscow's public baths, an inconvenience that most students apparently put up with every two weeks. Although university education is free in the Soviet Union for those few who qualify, Gorbachev, like most students, had to depend on a tiny stipend that barely covered his basic needs. To get by, he had to count on food parcels and whatever small funds he received from home as well as on what he could earn during the summer months back on the farm. These gifts were shared with others and they helped. Still, the students did not have an easy time. One former roommate recalled that by the end of the month all they had to live on was sweet tea and bread.

While Gorbachev lived like a typical student, he was unusual in that he was a country boy. Always dressed in his one ill-fitting suit, he was a misfit among the privileged and sophisticated young city people who predominated at Moscow State University. His field of study was law. This may not have been entirely by choice. Gorbachev had been a good high school student who did well in a number of subjects ranging from mathematics and physics to history and poetry. But he was not brilliant in any of them, which seems to have limited his choice of what he could study in Moscow. He ended up as a law student.

Law in Stalin's Soviet Union was not a prestigious

field. It was used mainly to keep the people in line, and often to terrorize them with harsh punishments. The legal profession offered few options. One could become a public prosecutor in what was called the procurator's office. Or one could enter the secret police and do similar work, but under cover and far more brutally. A very small number of law students—about 4 percent of the 1.2 million university students—did join the secret police.

Yet there were some important advantages to studying law, and Gorbachev, never one to miss an opportunity, would make the most of them. The law curriculum, like every other course of study in the Soviet Union, was saturated with propaganda. Marxism-Leninism was a requirement. It taught the usual Soviet propaganda line of that era: the evils of capitalism, the inevitability of its collapse, the virtues of socialism, and the perfection of the leadership of the living "genius" of Marxism, Joseph Stalin. The major texts stressed how Stalin's purge trials—when former top party leaders, after long and cruel torture, confessed to "crimes" of every conceivable nature they could not have possibly committed—were models of what was called "socialist legality."

The law curriculum also had some characteristics that made it unique in Soviet higher education. Law students studied subjects that gave them a broader view of the world. Roman law, international law, classical theories of the state, and the works of such thinkers as Thomas Aquinas, Thomas Hobbes, and Jean-Jacques Rousseau gave Soviet law students a glimpse of a world and way of thinking that few of their peers received. In addition, some of Gorbachev's law professors were nonparty members who had been trained before 1917. Of course, all Soviet educators had to be very careful to pay homage to the truth as defined by the Communist party. Still, because of the subjects they were teaching and their own backgrounds, something beyond the party line inevitably seeped into the education they gave to young people like Mikhail Gorbachev.

How this affected Gorbachev's thinking is difficult to know. For most students, whether Soviet or American, college years are a time of growth and change. Like Gorbachev, many college students are often away from home for the first time and have more independence than ever before. They get to know people from distant places, often for the first time. In Gorbachev's case this certainly was true. He became friendly with students not only from all over the Soviet Union, but from the newly communized countries of Eastern Europe. So it is quite likely that what Gorbachev's official biography calls his "inquiring mind,"[1] which is what has made him so special among Soviet leaders, was at least in part developed during his years as a law student.

There is one product of his law education that is obvious every time Gorbachev makes a speech or gives an interview. Soviet law students, like law students the world over, study how to present arguments, both orally and in writing. Gorbachev was already an articulate youth when he arrived in Moscow; five years of training must have made him a much better speaker. Most observers agree that he is the best speaker among leading Soviet politicians since the 1920s. He is often compared to Leon Trotsky, Lenin's closest associate after 1917, who was defeated by Stalin in the power struggle of the 1920s. Since Trotsky was a brilliant speaker, far better than Lenin, this comparison is very high praise. At any rate, Gorbachev would eventually become the first lawyer since Lenin to lead the Soviet Union.

The Soviet law course was intense and rigorous. Gorbachev and his peers had to commute to classes that ran six hours a day, six days a week. To miss any classes was to risk harsh punishment, including losing one's financial aid or even expulsion from the university. Most students had all they could handle to get to class and study their lessons after class. Not Gorbachev. He was bright enough to get his work done (and do well enough to earn an additional scholarship) so that he had time for other things. At the top of his list he worked to further his career by continuing his Komsomol activity. Even at a young age Gorbachev was not merely a law student, but a student of the Soviet system and how to get ahead in it. He recognized that the key was not only earning good grades but also showing loyalty and enthusiasm for party work and making the right connections in the party hierarchy. As one student acquaintance observed when Gorbachev became general secretary: "It was obvious he realized that party political activity would get him farther than his studies would."[2]

Gorbachev, then, while a student, was very much a man on the make. He worked hard as a Komsomol organizer at the law school. In 1951 he became one of the eleven members of the Komsomol governing committee there, and between 1952 and 1954 served as the top Komsomol official at the school. Meanwhile, beyond the confines of his school, he worked for the party committee in Moscow's Krasnaya Presnaya district, one of the most important party organizations in the capital. The connections he made there also undoubtedly helped his career.

Some payoffs, in fact, came relatively quickly. In 1951, Gorbachev was made what is called a candidate member of the Communist party. This is usually a one-year probationary period during which candidates are watched closely to see if they are suited for full party membership. This means showing total commitment and readiness to do whatever one is told. During the early 1950s this meant absolute loyalty and enthusiasm for Stalin and whatever he said or did. Obviously, Gorbachev demonstrated his love for his country's "Great Leader," as he became a full member of the party in 1952. Although he was now at the bottom of a pyramid of several million members, Gorbachev had become part of the elite group from which those who actually ran the Soviet Union were drawn.

Gorbachev's ambition and willingness to serve Stalin and the Soviet regime did not go unnoticed by his fellow students. Years later one of them commented that Gorbachev reminded him of "a good provincial actor who arrives at the capital and is doing well, but who constantly feels an inner need to prove himself, to assert himself on and off the stage."[3]

As was very much the practice in the Communist party, especially under Stalin, Gorbachev's self-promotion frequently damaged other people. He was a strict, sometimes brutal enforcer of the rules. Another former fellow student, Fridrikh Nezhansky, recalled "the steely voice of the Komsomol secretary of the Law Faculty, Gorbachev, demanding expulsion from the Komsomol for the slightest offense."[4] Another acquaintance adds that Gorbachev "played up incredibly to those in authority" and even supported Stalin's anti-Semitic campaign of the early 1950s.[5] It should therefore not be surprising that the same acquaintance recalls a friend pointing to Gorbachev and warning, "Be careful of him."[6]

At the same time, even those critical of Gorbachev remember being helped by him when they were victims of injustice, such as one of them being unfairly denied a job. And there appears to have been another side to Gorbachev, one that he revealed only to a few trusted friends. That was wise, since Gorbachev's other side was one that questioned some of what he saw, a dangerous habit under the Stalin that young Mikhail insisted he loved so much.

One of Gorbachev's roommates, to whom he did speak freely, was a student from Czechoslovakia named Zdenek Mlynar. That Gorbachev was allowed to room with Mlynar says a great deal, as only the most reliable Soviet students were trusted with that kind of exposure to foreigners. They were, in addition, expected to report on their roommates from Eastern Europe. And they were very carefully watched. When Mlynar sent his friend and roommate a postcard during the summer of 1951, it was personally delivered to Gorbachev in Privolnoye by a local police official.

Despite his unquestioned loyalty to the system, Gorbachev apparently did not believe everything he was told. He once told Mlynar that the official version of collectivization—that the peasants enthusiastically supported it and prospered enormously from the start—was inaccurate. Gorbachev also indirectly criticized Stalin's murderous treatment of his rivals by pointing out to Mlynar that Lenin did not have one of his political opponents, Julius Martov, executed or even arrested. Mlynar, who later would become a reformer in his native Czechoslovakia, only to be forced to leave his country after the Soviet Union crushed that movement with military force in 1968, added that:

> . . . in 1952 those words signified that the student Gorbachev doubted that there were only two types of Russians, those who adhered strictly to the Party line and the criminals who did not. What is more, to confide an opinion of this sort to a foreigner, even to a friend, was unusual in those days.[7]

Gorbachev in his university years thus seems to have been a young man with several "layers," as Mlynar put it, to his personality. He believed in the Soviet system and was determined to get ahead within that system. At the same time, he was capable of thinking for himself and arriving at unconventional conclusions. These were, however, not so radical that they undermined his basic communist beliefs. Nonetheless, since he understood the limits of what was permissible in his country, Gorbachev was careful enough to keep whatever unconventional views he had confined to a small group of trusted friends.

There was at least one other "layer" to Gorbachev in those days. He was a man who knew how to have a good time. That was not easy in Moscow in the early 1950s. There was little to do, and even less money to do it with. Occasionally someone would come up with a bottle of vodka. One of the more available forms of entertainment was, of all things, old American movies. They and other foreign films had been brought to the Soviet Union by the Soviet army, which had seized them when it occupied part of Germany at the end of World War II. Gorbachev also enjoyed the theater, and before long he was attending plays in the company of a young woman one year his junior named Raisa Titorenko.

Raisa was attractive and intelligent; she had won the gold medal, not the silver like Mikhail, upon graduation from secondary school. She was from a town near the city of Ufa in central Russia, the daughter of a railway engineer. Mikhail and Raisa met at a dancing lesson. Gorbachev actually was present only as a spectator, having gone there to poke fun at a friend who was taking the lesson. Raisa was also taking a lesson, and was introduced to Mikhail when it was over. They liked each other immediately and soon became a couple. Raisa, whose family was far better educated than that of her peasant boyfriend, played a major role in introducing Mikhail to Moscow's rich cultural life. In 1954 Raisa and Mikhail decided to get married. The wedding celebration took place in a dormitory cafeteria where, as one former classmate recalled, "everything was the cheapest." As was common at Russian weddings, most of the guests consumed too many alcoholic beverages and became drunk. Not the groom. As always, he drank very little and remained quite sober, a fitting gesture for the man who

Mikhail and Raisa Gorbachev in their younger years

thirty years later would launch a major campaign against his country's serious alcohol abuse problem.

Although getting married reflected their genuine youthful passion for each other, there were other factors pushing young couples like Mikhail and Raisa into matrimony. Simply put, it was almost the only way they could be together. Mikhail and his roommates usually scheduled an hour a week as "cleaning hours," when each of them had the private use of their room for an hour. An exception was made for Raisa and Mikhail's wedding night when "everyone had to disappear," as Mlynar recalls.[8] The Cinderella evening over, the young lovers returned to their old quarters for several months before being given their own space—a room, not an apartment—in a newly constructed dormitory for married students.

By the time Gorbachev graduated in 1955, major changes were taking place in the Soviet Union. Stalin's death two years earlier had led to more than just a political power struggle. Almost immediately after Stalin died, new policies emerged. The new Soviet leadership promised the people a higher standard of living, and even took a few small steps to provide more food and consumer goods. A very small number—a few thousands out of the millions—of the prisoners in the Gulag labor camps were released. Artists and writers were given more freedom to express themselves; one of the first products of this new freedom was a novel by Elya Ehrenburg called *The Thaw*, which gave its name to this period. The Soviet leadership also began to attempt to improve relations with the Western powers and thereby reduce international tensions.

At the same time a power struggle raged behind the scenes. It moved to center stage quickly, however, within months of Stalin's death. As army tanks rolled into Moscow, several of the new leaders combined to arrest and then to execute the man they all feared most, Lavrenti Beria, the head of the secret police. The struggle for power then came down to Georgi Malenkov versus Nikita Khrushchev. By the middle of 1955, just as Gorbachev was graduating and preparing to leave Moscow, Khrushchev emerged as the most powerful Soviet politician.

Unlike Khrushchev, Gorbachev seemed to have lost a political struggle of his own. Although Mikhail had done well in school and made many contacts through his political work, he was not selected for the Komsomol post he applied for in Moscow. Finally he accepted a position with the Komsomol in his native Stavropol. This position in the provinces, 1,000 miles (1,600 km) from the culture and excitement of Moscow, was far more modest than a Moscow State University law graduate would normally expect. Still, 1955 had its compensations. It was the year for Mikhail and Raisa to begin a new life, along with the rest of the Soviet Union, under the leadership of Nikita Khrushchev.

3
MAKING IT
IN STAVROPOL

When Mikhail Gorbachev returned to the Stavropol farming region in 1955, he did so to become a tiny cog in the huge political machine that governs the Soviet Union. That machine is often called the Soviet "party-state," the interlocking structure of the Soviet state and the Communist party. It is important to understand two facts about that structure. First, the Soviet state controls far more of the people's lives than does the government of any democratic country. That control is so absolute that Soviet society and societies similar to it are called "totalitarian" states. Second, the mighty Soviet state is in reality nothing more than a huge puppet. Its strings are pulled by a greater power: the Communist party of the Soviet Union.

The Soviet state and Communist party dominate virtually all aspects of Soviet life. The state owns all of the country's resources: its raw materials, factories, farmland, department stores, shops, and restaurants. And, most of what the state does not own it controls. For example, although collective farms supposedly own their tools and machines, the state actually controls them because the Communist party controls the collectives. A huge network of party-run organizations reinforces this control. These include labor unions, sports clubs, women's organizations, and many other groups that in democratic countries are run privately and independently. Lurking behind all this as an enforcer is the Soviet secret police, the KGB.

While this gigantic network is an effective controller, a huge and costly bureaucracy is needed to maintain it. Because so many important decisions are made in Moscow, local conditions are often ignored. For example, a collective farm in the village of Privolnoye is not free to decide what to produce. It is bound to decisions made in offices in Moscow over 1,000 miles (1,600 km) away, by officials who may know nothing about what grows best in those distant fields. The party and the state bureaucracies frequently overlap, so it often takes twice as long to get the work accomplished. The result is often inefficiency and wastefulness.

In Stavropol Gorbachev served in several branches of the all-encompassing Soviet political net. His first job was in the Komsomol organization responsible for the entire Stavropol region, which included the city of Stavropol and the surrounding 30,000 square miles (77,700 sq km). Gorbachev's official title was deputy head of the Department of Propaganda and Agitation. This made him the second-ranking official responsible for making sure the local youth believed everything the Communist party decided was the "truth." Later, when he moved up from the Komsomol to the Communist party, he first served in the branch of the party that ran only the city of Stavropol. Gorbachev then advanced to the party organization responsible for the entire Stavropol region.

When Gorbachev began his career in 1955, the Komsomol, as it does today, enrolled millions of young people ages fourteen to twenty-eight nationwide. It provided many forms of recreation to these youths, ranging from sports and hobbies to purely social events. The Komsomol's main task, however, has always been to build good Communists and servants of the state. According to its official rules, its job is:

to help the party educate youth in the communist spirit, to draw it into the work of building a new society, and to train a rising generation of harmoniously developed people who will live and work and administer affairs under communism.[1]

Komsomol members serve the community by helping with the harvest, repairing school equipment, and working with the aged. Boys undergo basic military training. All the while they are given heavy doses of propaganda. By the time they leave the Komsomol, most Soviet youths have accepted its values. A few of them, the most enthusiastic and best connected, people like Mikhail Gorbachev, enter the ranks of the Communist party.

Since 1985, General Secretary Gorbachev has been trying to change and to a degree dismantle the oppressive and suffocating totalitarian institutions that dominate Soviet life. In 1955, however, when he and Raisa returned to Stavropol, he just wanted to fit into the system. That system, of course, had changed in several important ways in the two years since Stalin's death. The most significant change was the curbing of the awesome power wielded by the secret police. The arrest and execution in 1953 of Stalin's head of secret police, Lavrenti Beria, brought the secret police under the control of the party, and not just one man. To the average Soviet citizen this meant that the terror and totally arbitrary arrests of Stalin's day were over. Soviet citizens still did not enjoy a lot of freedoms that citizens of democratic countries take for granted. But if they followed the rules, at least they were safe.

The Stavropol that greeted the Gorbachevs in 1955 was a pleasant town with a population of about 120,000. As one former resident recalls, it felt like an "overgrown agricultural village whose life centered entirely on a single street."[2] That main street, one of the literally thousands in the Soviet Union named after Karl Marx, was an attractive avenue graced by mansions built in the nineteenth century. Once the home of Stavropol's wealthy, they had been converted by the Bolsheviks to government use. The Gorbachevs eventually were able to settle into quarters that, while fairly modest, were far superior to the single small room they had in Moscow. The Gorbachevs' new residence, a green one-story building within walking distance of Gorbachev's office, had once been the home of a tsarist official.

Within a year they had their only child, a daughter they named Irina. Today she is an attractive and stylish woman whose facial features hint at the ethnic mixture characteristic of the Russian steppe. Irina is a physician married to a surgeon. They have two children. The oldest is a girl named Unexenia, who was born in the mid-1970s. The younger of Gorbachev's grandchildren, according to what he told former President Jimmy Carter, was born in 1987. Gorbachev seems to be a typically doting grandfather. He constantly showed pictures of his granddaughter while on a visit to Great Britain in 1984.

Neither the peaceful landscape of Stavropol nor his warm family life could calm the political turmoil in which Gorbachev had to work. One of the most important issues of the day was deciding the fate of an estimated 8 to 10 million Gulag prisoners. Most of them were Stalin's political victims; actually they were the lucky ones who had survived. Now they and their families were clamoring for their release. By 1955 there had even been several rebellions in the camps, which were cruelly put down. The Soviet government's legal arm, known as the procuracy, was swamped by family members of prisoners desperate to win freedom for their loved ones as quickly as possible. Because during the first few years after Stalin's death, releases were considered on a case-by-case basis, delays could last for years. This may have

The Gorbachevs' only child,
Irina, with her daughter

been a reason that Gorbachev did not choose to work in the procuracy, as most newly minted lawyers would have. In any case, as a lowly Komsomol official, Gorbachev could do little about the situation.

Then, on February 26, 1956, Khrushchev took a giant step into the unknown. The occasion was the Twentieth Congress of the Communist party, the first party congress since Stalin's death. As the congress was about to adjourn, Khrushchev called it back for a secret session. Then he delivered a four-and-one-half-hour speech in which he did the unthinkable: he criticized Stalin, and not gently, but harshly and bitterly. In doing so he shocked not only his audience, but the entire Communist world. Nobody knew for sure what would happen after Khrushchev shook the faith of millions of loyalists.

Khrushchev had a number of reasons for taking such a risk. He knew the terrible conditions under which the Soviet people lived. He was convinced that the prosperity communism promised his people could only be achieved if millions worked enthusiastically to build a better future. Yet he also knew that these millions did only what they had to, partly out of fear and partly because their work received little reward. To improve matters would require major reforms. But those reforms would be resisted by people throughout the party's ranks who had achieved their positions under Stalin and who feared that any significant change would threaten what they had. These people were powerful, and their case was backed by Stalin's unchallenged, god-like reputation. Khrushchev knew therefore that by attacking Stalin's reputation he would weaken his own opponents and clear the way for reform.

The speech was a huge political explosion. It sent out a flash of light that illuminated part of the Soviet political cosmos blackened by three decades of lies. Although Khrushchev left out much of the terrible truth about the Stalin years, some of which Gorbachev would begin to tell three decades later, he also told a great deal. Stalin had been a brutal dictator, Khrushchev insisted. He had murdered thousands of good, loyal party members during "mass repressions." He had blundered during World War II and caused the Soviet Union enormous losses. He had directed a reign of terror

> . . . *against the honest workers of the party and of the Soviet state; against them were made lying, slanderous, and absurd accusations concerning "two-facedness," "espionage," preparation of fictitious "plots," etc.* . . . *Confessions of guilt of many arrested and charged with enemy activity were gained with the help of cruel and inhuman tortures.*[3]

The "secret speech" did not remain secret for long. It was read in party meetings across the country, although it was not published for the general public. A copy of it did reach the West, where it caused a sensation. In the Soviet Union it caused far more than that. There it was nothing less than a crisis, not simply a political one, but for many party loyalists a crisis of faith. More than three decades later, in a speech in August 1987, Gorbachev would refer to his generation of party workers as the "children of the Twentieth Party Congress." By this he meant that the Twentieth Congress set the tone for the first serious effort at reforming the system Stalin had left behind, an effort Gorbachev and his associates were reviving years later. Gorbachev also had some other kind words for Khrushchev, to whom he has been compared both at home and in the West.

But in 1956 Khrushchev must have caused Gorbachev great difficulties. For a generation, Stalin had been looked upon as barely less than a god in the Soviet Union. In the West many people who had their faith shattered could and did leave the Communist party; those in the

51

Soviet Union had to come to terms with Khrushchev's revelations and continue their work. Like all party workers Gorbachev had been a convinced Stalinist. Even if the system had been hard on others, it had given Gorbachev's family a respected position in Soviet society and opened the way for Mikhail to attend Moscow State University. Now Mikhail Gorbachev, just starting his career, had to come to grips with information that contradicted many of his most cherished beliefs. He also had to explain the new truth to other party workers in meetings across the Stavropol region.

Khrushchev's "secret speech" began what is known as de-Stalinization. Khrushchev attempted a number of economic reforms and tried to make the party more responsive to the general public. There were initiatives to improve relations with the West, especially the United States. But de-Stalinization was uneven and full of contradictions. In the fall of 1956, impatience for greater change led to unrest that forced changes in the Soviet-controlled Communist government of Poland. The Polish crisis was followed by an outright rebellion against the Communist government of Hungary. That attempt to free Hungary from Soviet control was put down with Soviet tanks and troops at the cost of thousands of lives.

At home Khrushchev was criticized for going too far. In 1957 an attempt was made to unseat him by a group led by Malenkov. Khrushchev defeated his opponents and then turned his victory into another reform. Unlike Stalin, who had his defeated opponents killed, Khrushchev permitted his to take low-level jobs or to retire.

Gorbachev, who would face similar problems thirty years later, has never publicly discussed how he coped with the aftermath of Khrushchev's speech. Whatever his problems at the time, Gorbachev certainly must have welcomed much of the reform and experimentation of the Khrushchev era. What is certain is that Gorbachev made steady, though not spectacular, progress in his career. In 1956 he received his first promotion—he was appointed first secretary of the Stavropol city Komsomol organization. He was now the head of all Komsomol activity in the city of Stavropol.

It is important to understand how, at least after Stalin's death, one was promoted in the Communist party hierarchy. The key was to fit in, never to rock the boat, and to display loyalty to one's superiors and enthusiasm for all orders from above. It certainly helped to show some ability, but being a loyal party trooper came first. Playing by these rules was likely to attract the attention and support of someone higher up. As that superior moved up the ladder, one's own career prospered accordingly. Any person on the way up also needed loyal subordinates to cement his or her power. Therefore the first thing a party worker did upon assuming a new post was to try to move as many of his loyal followers as possible into key positions. This process went on at every level of the party.

Given Gorbachev's success, he must have played by those rules. He seems to have made sure to know what views to express at the proper time, and to never go out on a limb by himself. If he had been a committed Stalinist before 1953, he became an equally committed supporter of Khrushchev's policies in the mid-1950s and early 1960s. After Khrushchev's removal from office in 1964, Gorbachev followed the party line as laid down by Brezhnev and his supporters.

Gorbachev's first sponsor, and the man responsible for his first promotion in 1956, was the man who preceded him as secretary of the Stavropol city Komsomol organization, Vsevolod Murakhovsky. More important to Gorbachev was Fyodor Kulakov, who became head of the Stavropol regional Communist party organization in 1960. Kulakov was an effective and dynamic politician who eventually reached the Politburo, the small body

53

(usually composed of about ten to fifteen members) at the very top of the Communist party where the real decisions are made. Later came two other powerful figures: Mikhail Suslov and Yuri Andropov. Both had connections to the Stavropol region. The older, Suslov, was Stavropol's regional party leader from 1939 to 1944; Andropov was born in a local village, Nagutskaya. Despite the time they had spent in Stavropol, neither of the men had met Gorbachev, but both maintained an interest in the area and its politicians. Gorbachev seems to have been the politician who most impressed them.

In 1958 came a second promotion. Gorbachev was appointed second secretary, or the number-two man, in the regional Komsomol organization. Technically, Gorbachev was "elected" second secretary by the local organization. In reality, of course, these "elections" were arranged in advance by the party bosses higher up. Also, these "elections" had only one candidate. This system, which inevitably produced so much cynicism and apathy, was one of the most deeply rooted traditions in the Communist party. It also was one of the key mechanisms for enforcing Moscow's control on the country as a whole, and, years later, became one of the things that General Secretary Mikhail Gorbachev would try to change.

The political style that has since distinguished Gorbachev already was emerging by the 1960s. Gorbachev was not a man to sit behind a desk, as so many Soviet bureaucrats do. He preferred to see things first hand, to visit people and projects across the region and find out for himself how things were going. In doing this Gorbachev rejected Stalin's approach and instead followed Khrushchev's example. Gorbachev also tried to innovate, even while limited to the youthful world of the Komsomol. For example, he developed a very successful work/study program for students in Stavropol that other regions soon imitated. Khrushchev, of course, was far away in Moscow, so he could not pay attention to what a local official named Mikhail Gorbachev was doing in Stavropol. But this also was the style of Fyodor Kulakov, the man who ran the Stavropol region during the early 1960s, and who did know what Gorbachev was doing.

Kulakov arrived in Stavropol in 1960. For him his new job was a demotion. Kulakov, who held a degree in agronomy, the science of agriculture, was one of the people Khrushchev chose to blame for the country's poor agricultural performance. Consequently he lost his job in Moscow and was sent to serve in the countryside.

Kulakov did not let his demotion stop him. He was an active and able man who worked hard to make Stavropol a leader in Soviet agriculture. In the shake-up that accompanied the arrival of a new boss that year, Gorbachev moved up again. This time the promotion was substantial. Gorbachev became first secretary of the Komsomol regional organization. At the same time he got a foot in an important door. As the local Komsomol chief, he was made a member of the committee that ran the regional Communist party organization. In other words, Gorbachev now had a position in the organization with the real power, the Communist party, as well as at the top of the Komsomol, the junior organization.

Meanwhile, back in Moscow Khrushchev was still struggling with conservative forces that continued to block his reform efforts. In 1961 this led to a new assault on Stalin's memory, which Khrushchev hoped would discredit those who were resisting his programs once and for all. The occasion was the Twenty-second Party Congress in 1961. This time Gorbachev was important enough in Stavropol to be "elected" a delegate to the congress. The congress took place in a newly completed hall far larger than the one where previous congresses had met. Khrushchev filled it with over 5,000 delegates and invited guests. Then he put on a show that brought the house down.

This time Khrushchev did not even pretend to speak in secret. In front of the whole world he lashed out at Stalin as never before. The congress then took a symbolic, but very important step. Since his death Stalin's embalmed body had lain next to Lenin's in the Lenin Mausoleum in Moscow's central plaza, the famous Red Square. After a dramatic series of speeches, the congress voted to remove Stalin's body from the mausoleum and rebury it in another place inside the Kremlin, the ancient Moscow fortress that was the seat of the Soviet government. Since the vote, as usual, was unanimous, we can assume that Gorbachev supported the resolution. The triumph and tension of the moment were caught by a young Russian poet, Yevgeny Yevtushenko, who wrote:

Grimly clenching his embalmed fists,
just pretending to be dead, he watched from inside . . .
He was scheming. Had merely dozed off.
And I, appealing to our government, petition them
to double, and treble, the sentries guarding this
slab, and stop Stalin from ever rising again and,
with Stalin, the past.[4]

Stalin was reburied not under six feet of earth, but under several truckloads of concrete. All over the Soviet Union, statues of Stalin were toppled, monuments destroyed, and cities, towns, streets, and institutions of all kinds renamed. Stalingrad, the city where the great victory over the Germans that marked the turning point of World War II took place, did not escape the anti-Stalinist sweep. It was renamed Volgograd.

In spite of all the excitement caused by the Twenty-second Congress, Gorbachev's personal political life was rather dull. By 1962 Gorbachev, past thirty, was becoming old for the Komsomol, whose oldest members are only twenty-eight, even though its professional officials often are older than that. In March of 1962 a new opportunity opened up and Gorbachev took it. In Moscow Khrushchev was reorganizing his government, something he did several times. This time the party created new administrative units to supervise agriculture. There were hundreds of them all over the country, sixteen in the Stavropol region alone. Running one of these units was risky, especially for a man like Gorbachev. The new party units quickly found themselves in conflict with existing party organizations. Because the lines of responsibility were unclear, it was difficult to get many jobs done. Also, although Gorbachev had experience as a combine driver on a farm, he had no professional training in any other aspect of agriculture. Still, Gorbachev was offered one of the positions in the Stavropol region and he was bold enough to take it. At the age of thirty-one, he ended his Komsomol career to work exclusively with the big boys in the Communist party.

Gorbachev had several things going for him as he began his professional party work. Kulakov, the new boss in Stavropol, had noticed him and taken him under his wing. Gorbachev, meanwhile, went back to school. He enrolled as a correspondence student at the Stavropol Agricultural Institute. By getting a professional degree in agriculture, Gorbachev would be better able to do his job, and he would increase his chances of promotion. Taking one's degree as a correspondence student is quite common in the Soviet Union, especially for upwardly mobile party officials like Gorbachev. Finally, both Kulakov and Gorbachev benefited from the Stavropol region's healthy climate and picturesque countryside. There were a number of health resorts in the area, including the town of Kislovodsk and the hot springs at Mineral'nye Vody ("mineral waters") that were visited by top party leaders. Gorbachev had an opportunity to meet them and, as it turned out, to impress them.

In the sixties and into the seventies, however, Kulakov remained the key. It is quite possible that Gorbachev enrolled in the agricultural course to impress his boss in the classic way—by imitation. Kulakov, after all, held a degree in agronomy. But Gorbachev did more than imitate Kulakov. He went with him on many of his trips around the Stavropol region. He learned about its resources and problems directly, and undoubtedly reinforced his belief that a political leader could not lead hidden away in an office, but only if he got out and met the people.

Gorbachev and the rest of the Soviet people got a jolt in 1964 when Khrushchev was suddenly removed from office. He was deposed when the majority of the Presidium (as the Politburo was called from 1952 to 1964), led by Mikhail Suslov, organized against him. Suddenly Khrushchev, the country's honored leader for more than a decade, was denounced as a bumbler. Although he was allowed a comfortable retirement, all public mention of him ceased. Gorbachev and the rest of the Soviet people had to get used to their former leader becoming, in a matter of days, a virtual non-person. Along with Khrushchev went de-Stalinization and most reform efforts. Khrushchev's successor Leonid Brezhnev and his colleagues above all pursued the goal of stability. For those who would drink from the well of reform, Brezhnev's years in power would be a long dry spell.

Although Gorbachev may well have been among those who preferred continued reform, Khrushchev's fall did not hurt and even may have helped him. Gorbachev defended the decision to oust Khrushchev, even in private conversations with his friends. His reasoning followed the party line: Khrushchev had been a bungler. The plot that overthrew Khrushchev was hatched at a resort near Stavropol. It is likely that Kulakov, who officially would have hosted the meeting, knew about the plot, especially since he had a personal grudge against Khrushchev. And it is possible that Gorbachev, his trusted protégé, also understood what was going on, although he never has spoken of it.

At any rate, the early and mid-sixties were years of advancement for Gorbachev. In December of 1962, just months after his March promotion, he was given an important job managing party workers in rural parts of the Stavropol region. Gorbachev's luck remained good even after Kulakov left Stavropol in 1964, shortly after Khrushchev's fall. Kulakov was promoted to the post of party secretary in charge of agriculture. This post is attached to a powerful body known as the Secretariat of the Central Committee. The Central Committee is the party body just beneath the Politburo. Technically it elects the Politburo, although in fact greater power rests with the Politburo. But the Central Committee, which is made up of over 300 powerful officials from all over the country, is still a powerful body. Proof of this is that Khrushchev's overthrow could not be finalized until it received Central Committee support.

Back in Stavropol, Gorbachev got along well with the new local first secretary, Leonid Yefremov. Yefremov was an elderly man near the end of his career, so he was not an obstacle to the ambitions of a younger man like Gorbachev. He also was competent and an expert on agriculture. Gorbachev therefore continued to move up, partly because he now had a powerful sponsor, Kulakov, in Moscow itself. Although he was not a delegate to the party's Twenty-third Congress in 1966, Gorbachev did get a major promotion after the congress closed. He was made first secretary of the Stavropol city party organization. In effect, this made him the mayor of a city of over 170,000. In this post he was able to do something about improving the limited entertainment available in Stavropol. Although he received only discouragement from Moscow, Gorbachev was able to hustle, scratch, and scrape up the necessary funds to build his city a permanent circus. It is exactly this kind of initiative that is so rare in Soviet society. What Secretary General and President Gorbachev needs as much as anything today is more officials who work like Gorbachev did twenty years ago.

The next year, 1967, was one of academic achievement for the Gorbachevs. Mikhail received his degree from the Stavropol Agricultural Institute, and he was now what official Soviet publications call a "researcher agronomist-economist."[5] Soviet officials have stressed that Gorbachev insisted on taking his exams like any other student. The reality is a bit less inspiring: it is well known that party officials often go through the motions, and little else, when they get the correspondence course degree they need for advancement. It certainly is difficult to imagine the city's most powerful person being told he had failed by the Stavropol Agricultural Institute's director who, after all, was in effect one of Gorbachev's employees.

Raisa, meanwhile, received what is called a candidate of philosophic sciences degree, the equivalent of an American doctorate or Ph.D. Her rather unusual and quite interesting dissertation focused on the lives of collective farmers, in itself not an unusual topic. What distinguished it was that Raisa actually took the trouble to interview these farmers and find out what they thought, rather then just repeating worn-out party clichés. It is likely that her work had an effect wider than she or anyone expected. As Gorbachev told an American reporter when he was interviewed for U.S. television in 1987, he discusses all political matters with his wife.[6] So what Raisa found out about problems on the Soviet farms certainly reached her husband. And as he moved up the political ladder, his determination to solve the problems Raisa studied could be applied on an ever larger scale.

One other event of note occurred in 1967. Gorbachev was visited by his old university friend Zdenek Mlynar. By then Mlynar was a top party leader in his native Czechoslovakia. He told Gorbachev about the pace of reform and de-Stalinization in Czechoslovakia. In the Soviet Union, the rise of Brezhnev had brought a halt to de-Stalinization, but reform was moving ahead in Czechoslovakia. Gorbachev apparently was impressed with what Mlynar told him. But if Gorbachev envied his old friend in 1967, those feelings must have evaporated the following year, when the reform movement in Czechoslovakia went too far for the men in the Kremlin. In August 1968, thousands of soldiers from the Soviet Union and its Eastern European allies invaded Czechoslovakia. Those in power were removed, including Mlynar, who eventually emigrated to the West.

Gorbachev did much better than his former roommate in 1968. That year he became secretary of the Stavropol regional party organization, the territory's number-two man. This was significant because the pace of Gorbachev's career advanced; he had skipped over the post of third secretary. The following year brought mixed results. For decades Soviet agricultural planners had ignored the effects of their policies, such as the forceful tilling of semi-arid lands, on the environment. In 1969 the country experienced enormous dust storms, induced by drought. Damage was severe in the Stavropol region. As one Soviet agricultural expert has reported:

> *The whole* krai *[region] was extensively damaged by this natural disaster. The extensive system of irrigation canals became choked with dust. . . . drifts of soil, often more than two meters high, formed between the trees. . . . Villages and towns were covered with dust.*[7]

61

Gorbachev responded by becoming one of the first Soviet politicians to take an interest in the environment. That same year that the dust storms occurred he was elected to the Supreme Soviet, the Soviet Union's parliament. He then became a member of that body's environmental commission. The Supreme Soviet had no power and could only parrot party decisions, but it has some importance precisely because it did reflect party concerns.

In the meantime Gorbachev was learning something about the world outside the Soviet Union. His first trip abroad, in 1966, was to East Germany, one of the Soviet Union's Eastern European satellites. Later that year he made his first trip outside the Soviet bloc with a visit to France. Mikhail and Raisa were permitted to rent a car and tour France on their own for 3,000 miles (about 4,800 km), a privilege the Soviets give only to their most trusted officials. This was followed by a similar trip to Italy, which Gorbachev later recalled fondly.

> *This was a very interesting trip. We were in Sicily, near the small town of Terrazini. We made a bus tour of virtually the entire island, saw Etna . . . and visited the resort of Taormina. Then we traveled to other Italian cities, attended the L'Unità festival in Turin, and went to Florence and the small town of San Gimignano, nearby. I remember best the meetings we had in small towns and workers' settlements, with Italian workers.*[8]

These visits, and others, were more than pleasure trips. They taught Gorbachev a great deal about the West and seem to have made him comfortable in dealing with it. This did not mean very much in the 1970s, but after 1985 the lessons of Gorbachev's early travels were visible in the confidence and relaxed manner he brought to his diplomacy, impressing not only Western leaders, but millions of ordinary citizens in Western Europe and the United States.

In 1970 Gorbachev took his largest political step so far. Yefremov retired. Gorbachev was in an excellent position. He had done well as Stavropol's second secretary, and he had in Kulakov a powerful friend in Moscow. It therefore was no surprise that in April 1970, at the relatively young age of thirty-nine, Mikhail Gorbachev was "elected" first secretary of the Stavropol region. In effect he became the governor of over two million people. More importantly, he was the boss of one of the key agricultural regions in the Soviet Union. What he did now not only would affect his career, but would have an impact on his country as a whole.

4
THE STAVROPOL BOSS

During the 1970s Gorbachev's fortunes continued to rise. He began the decade as the local Stavropol party boss. He ended it as a Politburo member based in Moscow, one of the dozen most powerful men in his country.

The Soviet Union began the 1970s near the peak of its power. At home its standard of living was still increasing year to year, while its international power and influence was growing, in part due to its massive arms buildup. By the end of the decade much of this had changed. The Soviet economy and its standard of living had stagnated. Soviet industry, hamstrung by centralized planning that allowed almost no local initiative, was unable to adapt to the new technologies sweeping other industrialized countries. In agriculture, nothing seemed able to make the collective/state farm system work efficiently. Corruption in both economic and political affairs was rampant, as was cynicism, especially among the youth. On the international front, the Soviets faced growing problems with Poland, China, Afghanistan, and the United States and its Western European allies. Meanwhile, the Soviet leadership, symbolized by the sick and feeble Leonid Brezhnev, had grown old and incapable of responding to the growing challenges it faced. Several years later, Gorbachev summed up what he and many other Soviet citizens felt about that period when he called it the "era of stagnation."

In 1970, however, the future still looked bright. By making it to first secretary of the Stavropol region, Gorbachev became one the the Soviet Union's real elite. This was confirmed officially in 1971, when he became a full member (rather than a "candidate," or nonvoting member) of the Central Committee, the powerful party body second only to the Politburo.

The key to his future success was to please the Politburo in Moscow and to win as many powerful sponsors as possible who would want to advance his career. To do this Gorbachev had to make sure that the Stavropol region produced as much as possible, especially its all-important grain crop. He had to maintain order and make it clear that he was in complete control. And he had to make the right political moves in deciding which of the powerful Moscow party barons seemed strongest in the long run. To tie his fate to a loser in the constant struggles of the Soviet capital might cost him a demotion, and possibly his career.

Gorbachev had many rivals who also wanted to advance. The first secretaries in other regions of the RSFSR (Russian Soviet Federative Socialist Republic), such as the nearby Krasnodar and Rostov regions, were every bit as ambitious as Gorbachev. Another group of first secretaries on about the same level were those in the smaller Soviet republics. Among them was a man making a reputation for toughness and honesty during the 1970s—first secretary of the Georgian SSR Eduard Shevardnadze. Shevardnadze and Gorbachev probably met in the late 1950s. Gorbachev liked and respected Shevardnadze, and would later tap him to become his foreign minister.

During his Stavropol years Gorbachev emerged as a politician who knew when to toe the line and when to be daring and innovative. In some ways he was the traditional Soviet political boss, protecting his turf and those under him. One of his first moves as first secretary was to bring in his old patron Vsevolod Murakhovsky to head the Stavropol city party organization. Placing a loyal friend in that position was important to consolidating Gorbachev's political base. Gorbachev further protected himself by sheltering political allies who had committed offenses, at least when it was possible to do so. One important factor obviously was the seriousness of the offense. According to a former Stavropol official who later emigrated from the Soviet Union, Gorbachev, as first secretary of Stavropol city, once protected a subordinate who was charged with the theft of party funds.[1] But he did not try to protect an official accused of rape.

What made Gorbachev special, and a man to be reckoned with, was that he did much more than play the role of traditional party boss. He continued to go among the people, to travel his territory to see personally what was going on. His day, in fact, began that way. Most mornings First Secretary Gorbachev would walk the short distance from his home on Dzershinsky Street to his office on Karl Marx Prospect. It was easy for any citizen to greet the local party boss and, if so inclined, to inform him about what needed to be corrected in the region. Gorbachev tried to make the point that he was a man of the people in other ways. Once he canceled a formal dinner because he was invited to the home of a local worker who had won the Hero of Socialist Labor award, one of the Soviet Union's highest honors.

The North Caucasus in general and the Stavropol region in particular were important agricultural regions. It was therefore as a supplier of grain that Gorbachev had to excel if he expected to advance his career. One way was to encourage individual initiative by allowing the peasants more freedom to grow and sell privately, something the party leadership has frowned upon since collectivization. Here Gorbachev was simply following a local tradition. Private enterprise was tolerated in Stavropol more than in most areas of the Soviet Union.

This was in part because of tourism, a major local industry that had been growing dramatically since the 1950s. To keep visitors satisfied meant supplying them with good fresh food, especially fruits and vegetables. So the rules that governed what collective farmers could produce on their private plots and sell in private markets were relaxed, even to the point of bending official Soviet law and policy.

Another radical method to raise more food beyond the tiny area of the private plots was called the "brigade" system. In effect it involved turning entire fields over to groups called brigades, which would be entirely responsible for the planting and harvest, and would be paid according to what they produced. According to Gorbachev, "As a rule, these teams obtain 20 to 30 per cent more produce from a given area, with lower outlays of labour and resources."[2] In other words, when farmers were paid fairly for what they produced, they worked harder and got more results.

The system worked well enough to be expanded officially to the entire Stavropol region by the middle of the decade. The only problem was that it inevitably created richer and poorer farmers. In capitalist societies, different degrees of wealth based on productivity are considered normal. But allowing such differences violates the basic values of the socialist Soviet Union. Although differences in wealth and living standards exist there, and are often quite extreme, they still are discouraged and, as far as possible, denied. Gorbachev therefore soon found himself seeking other methods of raising production that were more in tune with accepted practice and official socialist ideology.

Back in Moscow, Kulakov, as party secretary in charge of agriculture, was engaged in the same search. In 1977 he came up with what was called the Ipatovo method, named after the district in which it was first tried. The Ipatovo method was a throwback to the old methods of

Large grain combines
ply the fields of a
state farm as Soviet
farmers implement the
Ipatovo method, developed
by party secretary in
charge of agriculture
Fyodor Kulakov (left).
Kulakov was a powerful
friend and mentor
of Gorbachev's.

amassing huge resources to solve a problem. This time what was amassed was a huge quantity of agricultural machinery and people. The goal was to cut the time it took to harvest grain, since it was felt that the slow pace of the harvests on the collectives led to large losses of grain through spoilage.

The whole project took on the look of a military campaign, with entire fields covered by huge steel vehicles. There were harvesters, trucks, mobile showers, and even mobile houses so crews could be in the field around the clock. Nothing was left to chance; along with repair units and other support groups there were "ideological" teams to boost morale. To make sure that the farmers' enthusiasm did not wane, the work teams were paid according to what they harvested. No thought was given to what all this cost. But since food in the Soviet Union is subsidized by the state—in other words sold to consumers for less than the cost of producing it—that factor could be ignored.

The results in the short term were encouraging. The harvest was completed in nine days, and a record amount of grain was delivered to the state. Kulakov could bask in the glory of his success. To a lesser degree, befitting his lower rank, so could Gorbachev. His reward was his first appearance in *Pravda,* the official newspaper of the Communist party and the leading newspaper in the Soviet Union. On July 17, 1977, in his most important press interview so far in his career, Gorbachev had the opportunity to say all the right things, and on page one of *Pravda,* no less. He pointed out that the harvesters had overcome many difficulties. It had rained almost every day, for example. But, stressed the proud Stavropol first secretary, his regional party organization took measures "to harvest the grain without losses." This meant a "stream of Stavropol bread is accumulating in the granaries of the nation."[3]

The awards came streaming in as well. Gorbachev won

the prestigious Order of the October Revolution. A few months later, so did the city of Stavropol. These awards acquired even more status when Mikhail Suslov, the second most powerful political figure in the Soviet Union, came to Stavropol to present Gorbachev with his award. That was quite a birthday present for Gorbachev, who turned forty-seven the day after the ceremony.

Alas, the grain stream of Stavropol soon ran dry, as it did elsewhere in the Soviet Union. The Ipatovo method was an enormous effort that could not work effectively over the long term. This was true for the Stavropol region, and even more true for the gigantic Soviet Union as a whole. The old problems of mismanagement, lack of incentives, and unreliable weather reasserted themselves. The 1978 harvest, and every harvest until Brezhnev died in 1982, was poor. Among the projects buried by this avalanche of bad harvests was the Ipatovo method. In 1983, once Brezhnev's death made more open criticism possible, the important newspaper *Izvestia* had this to say about Ipatovo:

> *All those fleets of machinery set up by the Ipatovo method. . . . All the machines are concentrated in large units, often unnecessarily. And then a whole armada of farm machinery rolls off in one direction or another because conditions are right for harvesting a few fields—when two combine harvesters would be enough. And on the other hand there are fields which cannot be harvested until the fleets of machinery have completed their tasks elsewhere.*[4]

All this time Gorbachev brought his innovative and open style to other aspects of his job. He made the most of his superb speaking skills, making countless speeches to party workers and ordinary citizens all over the region. He was far more open and frank with the local press than other regional bosses, and encouraged journalists to be more independent than was customary. He also continued to travel abroad to Western Europe, a sign that his work was appreciated in Moscow. In 1972 he went to Belgium, in 1975 to West Germany, and in 1976 to France, this time as the head of a Soviet group of visitors.

At home Gorbachev continued his interest in the environment, especially as it affected agriculture. Once, Gorbachev intervened to prevent a road construction project that would have destroyed a hilly area where a rare type of grass grew. In another instance he campaigned for an improved tractor design. This was a more formidable undertaking. Gorbachev had to challenge the Soviet military because many Soviet tractors are made in military factories that also produce tanks. These tank-based tractors are very heavy, and as they rode over the fields they compacted the soil, causing it to become too hard to absorb adequate water. After a long battle Gorbachev won a small concession. The old cumbersome design was retained and production at the army's factories was not disrupted. However, wider tires were installed on the tractors to spread the machines' huge weight over a larger area and thus reduce damage to the soil.

While doing the best he could in Stavropol, Gorbachev kept a close eye on experiments Eduard Shevardnadze was trying in Georgia with less centralized economic management that allowed for more individual initiative. At the same time others were keeping their eyes on Gorbachev, who was developing a reputation for competence and honesty. A politician's reputation, however, was not enough. It was also necessary to make the right personal connections. Gorbachev benefited from the Stavropol resorts, which continued to draw Moscow's top leaders for rest and relaxation. By the 1970s several top elderly leaders were coming to Stavropol often because of continuous health problems. So, in a sense, their age and bad health was Gorbachev's good fortune. Gorbachev met Alexei Kosygin, the powerful Politburo member mainly responsible for the nation's economy. Suslov also saw Gorbachev during his Stavropol vacations. Most of all, Gorbachev got to know Yuri Andropov. Andropov became head of the secret police, the KGB, in 1967 and grew more powerful every year. He and his fellow Stavropol native Mikhail Gorbachev became very friendly. They often took long walks together in the woods near the resort where Andropov stayed. Gorbachev was becoming Andropov's protégé.

It turned out that Gorbachev would need these men more than he might have expected. In early July of 1978, Feodor Kulakov, the youngest, most vigorous, and possibly the most intelligent Politburo member, died suddenly. The official report said nothing more than that his "heart stopped beating."[5] This non-explanation naturally led to rumors. It is likely that Kulakov had a falling out with Brezhnev, and that the party boss planned to blame him for agricultural problems and demote him. It has been suggested that because of this Kulakov committed suicide. But this rumor is impossible to prove and difficult to believe. There certainly was some kind of problem at the Politburo, as Brezhnev, Suslov, and Kosygin, the top three party bosses, did not attend Kulakov's funeral. It was chaired by Andrei Kirilenko, another Politburo member, who gave the main eulogy.

Gorbachev also spoke. His short speech was printed in its entirety in *Pravda,* the first time he received such an honor. Most of it was standard for Soviet funerals. Gorbachev observed that "our party, the entire Soviet people accompany on his last journey . . . Feodor Davidovich Kulakov." He noted that Kulakov was a "son of the Leninist party" and a product of "the working people." But at the very end of his speech Gorbachev suddenly changed his tone. Although Kulakov may have fallen out with Brezhnev, Gorbachev made his loyalty and affection for his mentor clear with an emotional closing: "Farewell, dear friend and comrade."[6] It was a demonstration of emotion, and possibly courage, not often seen at these ceremonies.

Kulakov's death might have been a setback for Gorbachev. Thanks to Andropov, it turned out to be the reverse. Kulakov's death created a vacancy in the job of Central Committee secretary responsible for agriculture. At the same time, the death of a powerful Politburo member intensified political maneuvering among that body's factions. It appears that Brezhnev had his own candidate for the agriculture job. He also wanted to promote his associates in the Politburo. One of them was Konstantin Chernenko, who several years later would actually become general secretary. But Brezhnev seemed to have run into opposition from several men, including Suslov and Andropov.

Negotiations and maneuvering went on for several months. At one point Suslov, Kosygin, and Andropov all vacationed in Stavropol. These visits make it almost certain that Gorbachev was involved in the discussions about his future. Then Brezhnev, accompanied by his friend Chernenko, toured part of the southern Soviet Union in September. His trip brought him to the Stavropol resort of Mineral'nye Vody, where Gorbachev met him at the train station. Since Andropov was vacationing in the area, he also showed up. And so four current or future general secretaries—Brezhnev, Andropov, Chernenko, and Gorbachev—found themselves together on a small resort train station 1,000 miles (1,600 km) from Moscow.

The meeting must have gone well. By the end of November arrangements were finalized. Brezhnev got the Politburo slots for his friends, including full membership for the loyal Chernenko. Mikhail Gorbachev was designated as the Central Committee secretary responsible for agriculture. Once again, Gorbachev had taken on a job that was not going to be easy. But it was the job that brought him back to Moscow.

5
RETURN TO MOSCOW

In 1950, when Mikhail Gorbachev arrived in Moscow
for the first time, the mood in the capital was tense and
the country was poised for change. A period of uncer-
tainty and a struggle for power followed Stalin's death
three years later. A dynamic new leader named Nikita
Khrushchev then emerged. He removed many of Stalin's cronies from office and led the country through a
era of reform and revitalization.

In 1978, when Gorbachev returned to Moscow, a
similar process was about to begin. Leonid Brezhnev, in
power since 1964, was in failing health. In the late 1970s
the Soviet Union was in a rut as large as itself. Brezhnev
and most of the Soviet Union's top leaders had grown
old and lacked vitality. The country's economy was slug-
gish. Corruption was widespread, from lower- and
middle-level officials all the way up to the Kremlin. A
black market economy that provided Soviet citizens with
many of the goods the official economy could not produce was thriving. Cynicism was growing as well among
many highly trained intellectuals and among the young.

The next several years made things worse. The harvests were poor. In 1979, the Soviet army was sent into
neighboring Afghanistan to prop up a collapsing Communist regime that a year earlier had seized power with
Soviet help. The invasion also led to an American grain
embargo against the Soviet Union and a boycott by many

Western nations of the Olympic Games, held in Moscow in 1980. That same year also brought a crisis in Poland. The Communist government there was corrupt, inept, and totally lacking in public support. In 1980 poor economic conditions led to a series of massive strikes and the birth of an independent labor movement called Solidarity.

The Soviet government, with an increasingly feeble Brezhnev at the helm, did little but sit tight as the situation worsened. For many of its citizens it was a period of frustration and embarrassment.

While Gorbachev certainly must have shared some of those feelings, he was too busy to have much time to dwell on them. On a personal level, he and Raisa were once again able to enjoy the cultural life of the capital: ballet, theater, and other forms of entertainment unavailable in the provinces. On the professional and political level, Gorbachev had far more to keep him busy. As the Central Committee secretary in charge of agriculture, he had one of the most difficult and thankless jobs in the Soviet Union. Agriculture is the area in which the Soviet centralization of decision-making and power is most destructive. In the Soviet Union, thousands of critical decisions—the kind that American farmers make on the spot in response to local needs—are made in Moscow. Moscow bureaucrats, not local farmers, decide what to plant, often setting targets ten years into the future. They decide what roads to build, which machines to produce, what fertilizers are needed, and the prices for everything from grain to tractors to animal feed. These decisions often ignore local needs and conditions and result in waste and inefficiency. At the time they were made in more than twenty ministries and committees scattered across Moscow, which inevitably added to the chaos. It was Gorbachev's job to do what nobody had done before, to make this unmanageable system work.

Gorbachev tried hard, but he did not succeed. During the years he was in charge of agriculture, every harvest was disappointing. Some were disasters. The grain figures tell the sad story. After the record harvest in 1978 of 230 million tons, the numbers plunged to 179 million tons in 1979, 189 million tons in 1980, 155 million tons in 1981, and 175 million tons in 1982. These figures were so bad that the last two were kept secret from the Soviet people. Gorbachev did suggest some reforms in 1981. He wanted to ease the restrictions of the farmers' private plots and introduce incentives to encourage more individual initiative. But his plans, like so many other attempts to loosen the Soviet economy, went nowhere. The only major initiative of those years was the "Food Program" of 1982, the last year of Brezhnev's life. It involved a huge commitment of money and effort, but did almost nothing to let the *farmers* decide what to plant and what to charge for their crops. As one expert described it,

> *Never had so many decisions and decrees about agriculture been made within a single year. None of them made much difference. . . . The program was the single largest, most expansive document ever produced on agriculture, but it was also the least imaginative. It has not worked because it is not a* reform.[1]

While Gorbachev may have failed as a food provider, he was successful as a politician. Under ordinary circumstances, he might have been made the scapegoat for the continued agricultural failures, to take the heat off Brezhnev and other top leaders. He wasn't, partly because it made no sense to blame one man for the failure of the system and, more importantly, because the men who had brought Gorbachev to Moscow continued to protect him. In addition, Gorbachev had established a reputation of being a cooperative and honest party man, and he had the ability to get along with those who counted. It helped that he also kept a low profile and stayed in the background.

So Mikhail Sergeyevich Gorbachev, who ranked about twentieth among the top Soviet leaders in 1978, moved up the slippery top rungs of the party ladder. In November 1979, at the age of forty-eight, he became a candidate, or nonvoting member, of the Politburo. He became a full Politburo member exactly a year later. It had taken Gorbachev barely a year to make a political leap that normally takes much longer. At forty-nine, he was by far the youngest member of a body made up largely of men old enough to be his father. The average age of the Politburo membership was over seventy, and many of them were in poor health. Not only had Gorbachev become one of the dozen most powerful men in his country, but he was one of the few in that group who was young and vigorous enough to do something positive with that power.

It was not only his age that made Gorbachev different from most of his colleagues. In 1981 he gave an interview to John Chrystal, an American businessman who knew the Soviet Union and its leadership very well. Although he found that Gorbachev believed many of the Soviet myths about "huge armies of the near starving" in the United States, the American noticed right away that Gorbachev seemed more direct and eager to learn than most other Soviet leaders.

> *There was a presence about him. He gave the impression of being a guy who was forming a vision, and had self-confidence and perseverance. He just wouldn't let a subject go until you were done.*[2]

By 1981 something was, slowly, beginning to let go in the Soviet Union: the Brezhnev era. Two forces were at work: time and Yuri Andropov. Time was taking its toll on the old men in the Kremlin. Alexei Kosygin, a top leader whom Brezhnev had pushed into retirement in October 1980, died that December. Early in 1982, Mikhail Suslov, a power in Soviet politics since the 1950s, also died. Brezhnev, who had not always agreed with Suslov but who had worked with him for many years, wept openly at the funeral on a freezing Moscow January day. Two months later Brezhnev himself suffered a stroke, his second, that brought him close to death.

By the spring of 1982 Brezhnev had recovered sufficiently to resume some of his official duties. But Yuri Andropov was busy working against him. Andropov served as head of the KGB from 1966 to 1982. He therefore knew many of the Soviet Union's secrets, including problems in the economy and the corruption of many of its leaders. He knew that corruption had reached the Kremlin and members of Brezhnev's family. Tough, ruthless, and totally committed to shaking things up, Andropov was determined to do something to get his country on track again.

He also was determined to become general secretary. To accomplish these goals Andropov had to build his political base beyond the KGB. That was the reason he gave up his KGB post to move over to the Secretariat in 1982. One source of support was the military, which was worried about the Soviet Union's ability to maintain its military strength in the face of a weakening economy. Another source was a group of younger party politicians favoring change. The most visible of them, though by far not the only one, was Gorbachev. It was largely thanks to Andropov, who worked to increase the stature of his protégés, that Gorbachev was promoted so quickly after 1978 and was given the prestigious Order of Lenin award in 1981.

Beginning in 1980 stories about corruption in high places that were embarrassing to Brezhnev began to leak to the press. A campaign was launched against corrupt officials associated with Brezhnev and several lost their jobs. The source of all this was Andropov. In the back rooms of the Kremlin, a political struggle between Andropov's and Brezhnev's supporters had broken out. The latter group was led by Chernenko, the man Brezhnev hoped would succeed him. One of the casualties in the struggle might well have been Gorbachev, since by 1982 Brezhnev probably was planning to make him the scapegoat for the latest agricultural failures.

Brezhnev would create no new scapegoats. On November 10, 1982, he died of a heart attack. Chernenko was the logical choice to replace him. But Andropov had done his work well. Backed by a majority of the Politburo, which included Defense Minister Dmitry Ustinov and Foreign Minister Andrei Gromyko as well as Gorbachev and several others, Andropov was elected general secretary the day after Brezhnev's death. The time had come for change, as well as for Mikhail Gorbachev to play a major and visible role in the process.

On November 10, official announcements told the nation that their late leader "will live forever in the hearts of the Soviet people and the entire progressive mankind." At Brezhnev's funeral, Andropov had praised him as the "flesh of the flesh and the bone of the bone of the people."[3] Actually, Andropov's goal was to discredit Brezhnev so he could clean up the mess he believed Brezhnev's laxness and corruption had caused. It is important to understand how Andropov planned to do this. Rather than loosen controls, he wanted to tighten them. To Yuri Andropov reform meant increased discipline and order, not more democracy or other ideas that might come from the West. Andropov, if anything, was more hostile to the West than Brezhnev. During Andropov's brief fifteen months in office, relations with the United States became even worse than they had been during Brezhnev's last years.

*Top party officials,
photographed in 1981.
Second row, left to right:
Chernenko (first), Suslov
(third), and Brezhnev (fourth);
third row: Gorbachev (first);
fourth row: Andropov (third)
and Gromyko (fourth).*

Andropov's tough approach quickly became clear. A new age of discipline had arrived. Shoppers taking time off from work to stand on long lines to buy scarce consumer goods were arrested. Andropov sent the police into bars, and even into public baths, to collar truants from work. Few people were immune; among those routed from their Turkish baths on one occasion were several army generals. There were thousands of arrests of people engaged in illegal black market activities. Official corruption also came under fire and many people were arrested. Harsh sentences were handed out, including the death penalty. Meanwhile Andropov replaced many long-term party and government officials with younger people who he expected would be more honest, vigorous, and efficient.

Andropov's goal was to revive the economy. He did have some short-run successes. During 1983, industrial production rose about 4 percent. Grain production rose over 10 percent, although it still fell 20 percent short of the official target. But Andropov's reliance on more discipline and force frightened many people. Others simply ignored his calls to work harder, since there were few rewards for additional efforts. Most Soviet workers continued to follow their old slogan: "They pretend to pay, we pretend to work."

Someone who was working, and very hard at that, was Mikhail Gorbachev. He was one of only four men who sat on both the Politburo, where the most important decisions were made, and the Secretariat, where responsibility lay for carrying out those decisions. During Andropov's short term in office Gorbachev emerged as a political power of the first rank and a public figure who was nationally and internationally known. He became one of the three or four most powerful Politburo members. He also was recognized as Andropov's number one ally and enforcer.

Signs of Gorbachev's influence were visible in agricultural policy. Early in 1983 a plan surfaced to allow farmers more freedom to raise cows and pigs on their private plots. In March of that year, Gorbachev made a speech in which he suggested that, to encourage harder work, the state give farmers long-term contracts based on what they produce. In the summer a document that went well beyond agriculture to the economy as a whole was leaked to an American reporter. It was called the "Novosibirsk Report," after a major research community in western Siberia. The report caused a sensation. It asserted the need for a "restructuring which would reflect fundamental changes" in the economy, including a greater reliance on "market relations." These were code words for a free market.[4] Gorbachev may have been involved in publishing this report, as after 1985 several specialists from Novosibirsk emerged among his advisors, including the report's author, Tatyana Zaslavskaya.

There were other, more substantial signs of Gorbachev's growing importance. During 1983 he gave up his post as party secretary for agriculture to become secretary in charge of ideology. The importance of this move was unmistakable. Ideology occupies a position in Communist states similar to that of dogma in religion. Within the Communist party of the Soviet Union, the ideology post is second in importance only to that of the general secretary. For many years Suslov had held the job; now Andropov gave it to Gorbachev.

Another clear sign of Gorbachev's power emerged when he was given the responsibility for selecting personnel for key party jobs. Gorbachev, in effect, became the manager of Andropov's housecleaning. It was a major undertaking. In party "elections" Gorbachev managed for Andropov in February 1984, about 15 percent of all regional secretaries (the job Gorbachev himself had held in Stavropol between 1970 and 1978) were replaced. This strengthened Andropov's campaign for reform. Since Gorbachev was in charge, it obviously expanded his power base as well.

Meanwhile Westerners were getting their own first-hand look at the rising young Soviet political star. In May 1983 Gorbachev led a Soviet delegation on a ten-day tour of Canada. The trip took him across Canada, from its Parliament in Ottawa in the east to a chow line on a ranch in the western province of Alberta. He spoke with Canada's prime minister and with ordinary workers and farmers. He ate lunch atop the CN Tower in Toronto, the highest freestanding structure in the world, and went on a boat ride beneath the raging waters of Niagara Falls. When Gorbachev spoke to factory workers, he questioned them carefully about the day-to-day details of their lives. When it was his turn to be questioned, he was not afraid of difficult questions posed by Canada's members of Parliament. He spoke about Afghanistan, human rights for Soviet citizens, and nuclear disarmament. Even as he delivered the party line, Gorbachev impressed his hosts as an able politician.

When Gorbachev returned home he found his political skills were about to be tested as never before. In the middle of 1983 Andropov's health suddenly deteriorated. He was suffering from kidney disease and by summer he was hospitalized. Gorbachev became one of the few non–family members to see Andropov regularly. This naturally increased Gorbachev's importance. But it was very difficult to run the Soviet Union with a sick man in charge. An important Central Committee meeting scheduled for the fall to discuss promotions to top-level party positions had to be postponed. It finally convened in December, when Andropov told his colleagues to meet without him since "for the moment" he was unable to take part.[5] Barely two months later, Andropov was dead of kidney failure.

It took four days to select a successor to Andropov. Neither of the two leading candidates won out. They were Gorbachev and Grigori Romanov. Romanov, only eight years older than Gorbachev, was the former party boss in Leningrad whom Andropov had brought to Moscow. His reputation for toughness and ruthlessness had earned him the nickname "Little Stalin." Because neither Gorbachev nor Romanov could manage a majority in the Politburo, Konstantin Chernenko, passed over only fifteen months earlier, was chosen as general secretary.

Chernenko, whose health was barely better than Andropov's, was only a caretaker. He suffered from emphysema, a disease that makes breathing difficult. At Andropov's funeral the frail Chernenko could barely get through his speech. He was too weak even to raise his arm for a proper salute to military units as they marched by. In effect, his selection was the last stand of the Brezhnev old guard.

During Chernenko's brief term, Gorbachev became the unofficial second-in-command. At one point *Pravda* referred to him as the "second secretary." That post did not exist, but it was clear that Gorbachev increasingly was running the show as Chernenko staggered from day to day. Despite Gorbachev's prominence, he was still not the party leader. Under Chernenko the pace of reform clearly slowed down, and in some cases was reversed. One important step was taken, however, that proved to be an indicator of things to come. In the fall the Soviets and Americans announced that they would resume talks on arms control, which had fallen apart under Andropov. This clearly was Gorbachev's doing. Since the middle of the year he had been chairman of the Foreign Affairs Commission of the Supreme Soviet. He had publicly advocated improved Soviet-American relations. In one speech, for example, Gorbachev had called for "an honest dialogue with real content, serious negotiations on the basis of equality and real security."[6]

Gorbachev got his chance to talk directly to the West when he visited Great Britain in December of 1984. This time, however, he shared the spotlight with his wife, Raisa. To Westerners accustomed to seeing lumpy old-fashioned Soviet wives who looked like peasants and stayed in the background—if they were visible at all—Raisa was a stunning new experience. She was fashionable, slender, outspoken, and obviously extremely intelligent and well informed. She could speak with authority on subjects dear to the British, such as Shakespeare. At the same time, she impressed her hosts as being totally up-to-date when she shopped in London's most exclusive shops and department stores, using her American Express Gold Card.

Mikhail meanwhile was putting on his own show. He toured widely and discussed vital world problems openly. He did not flinch when challenged on human rights, despite the Soviet Union's harsh treatment of dissidents and Soviet Jews who were being denied the right to emigrate from the country. In response to a question about religious freedom, Gorbachev countered with a statement about British problems in Northern Ireland, ending with the widely quoted remark: "You govern your society and we'll govern ours." He impressed people across the spectrum of British political life. A member of the opposition Labor party said of Gorbachev:

> *He is a man of exceptional charm with a relaxed, self-deprecating sense of humor. Emotions flicker over a face of unusual sensitivity like summer breezes on a pond. In discussions he was frank and flexible with a composure full of inner strength.*[7]

More importantly, Prime Minister Margaret Thatcher of the governing Conservative party observed, "I like Mr. Gorbachev. We can do business together."[8]

Mrs. Thatcher would soon get her chance. Barely two months after Gorbachev returned home, Konstantin Chernenko died after only thirteen months in office. There was a short struggle over the succession when Romanov tried unsuccessfully to put together a coalition to stop Gorbachev in the Politburo. The Politburo endorsed Gorbachev. The next day the Central Committee confirmed that decision. The official nominating speech was given by Andrei Gromyko, the longtime foreign minister and the most powerful remaining member of the Brezhnev generation.

"Comrades, this man has a nice smile, but he has iron teeth," Gromyko told the Central Committee. Whether that phrase, which was stricken from the official version of Gromyko's speech, was a warning or compliment is unknown. When Gorbachev was asked later by a Western reporter if in fact he had iron teeth he replied: "No, fortunately I have all my teeth."[9] He would need every one, and all the good fortune he could muster, to handle the immense challenge he had just bitten off: the task of reforming the Soviet Union.

6
THE GENERAL SECRETARY

The events of March 1985 brought a new general secretary into power and in so doing turned the job of
running the Soviet Union over to a new generation of
politicians. These were people whose experiences were
very different from the aging Brezhnev men. The old
leaders had participated in the industrialization drive, lived
through the purges of the 1930s, fought in World War
II, and run the Soviet Union since the death of Stalin.
For most of the people around Gorbachev, the industrialization of the Soviet Union was not something they
helped to bring about—it was an established fact. Like
Gorbachev, most were too young to have fought in
World War II. They had begun their careers during the
early Khrushchev years, and were influenced by the spirit
and possibilities of those times. Gorbachev and his colleagues were the first Soviet leaders, with the exception
of Lenin and some of his associates, to have a formal
university education. They also benefited from the rising
Soviet standard of living during the 1960s and 1970s.
They enjoyed the opportunity to visit and learn about
the West. This had made many of them comfortable with
Westerners and less afraid to borrow both methods and
ideas from the United States and Europe.

Actually, the Gorbachev generation is part of a larger
change in Soviet society that evolved between Stalin's

death in 1953 and Gorbachev's selection as general secretary more than thirty years later. During that period, industry grew and increasingly dominated the Soviet economy. Cities became bigger, turning the Soviet Union into a heavily urbanized society. More people than ever before received secondary and higher education. These skilled specialists—scientists, engineers, economists, and experts in many other fields—became vital to running the country. Without them the Communist party bureaucracy simply could not keep things going. In effect, although the party dominated the Soviet political system, a certain amount of power inevitably slipped from its hands as the Soviet Union modernized.

This increasingly skilled and aware element of the population gradually became frustrated with the inefficient way the party ran the country. Thus people used their skills and modern technology to find their way around party controls. For example, tape recorders, often smuggled in from abroad, became a handy way of transmitting information. This information could be a statement by a dissenter in prison or a rock song the authorities refused to record in the state-controlled studios. What was developing over time, between the bosses at the top and the workers and peasants at the bottom, was what in the West is called a middle class. It mattered little that the existence of such a class in the Soviet Union was impossible according to Marxist theory. The new Soviet middle class even had many of the values of the Western middle class. It wanted a higher standard of living; the right to read, view, or hear what it wanted; and the freedom to learn about the outside world.

Many of these people were party members, and some of them were moving up the ladder of power. These people knew as well as anyone how inefficient and stagnant Soviet life had become under Brezhnev. In short, an increasingly important part of Soviet society wanted to change the way the country was governed, how its economy was organized, how information was distributed, and much more.

Mikhail Gorbachev understands how his country has changed. He knows that he is the product of a broad, long-term, and unstoppable process. As he told foreign journalists in 1987:

> *I disagree with what is sometimes said, that the way toward the renewal of Socialism is personally associated with the name of Gorbachev. That would be a contradiction of the truth. The forming of the new course is an expression of the fact that Soviet society and the Soviet people have gained an extensive understanding of the need for change. In other words, if there were no Gorbachev there would have been someone else. Our society is ripe for changes, and the need for change has cleared its own road.*[1]

Although there is much truth in this statement, Gorbachev may have underestimated his own importance. Since 1985 he has demonstrated to millions at home and abroad that he is immensely gifted in many ways and would be very difficult to replace. Still, he is correct in pointing out how the Soviet Union has changed a great deal in the past generation. Without those changes, it would have been impossible for a man like Mikhail Gorbachev to reach the top. Once there, it would have been impossible for him to introduce reforms. The reforms could only be happening in a Soviet Union where decades of evolution had first prepared the stage for change. Gorbachev had the luck in 1985 to be the right man in the right place when the times were ripe in the Soviet Union for a man with his goals and talents.

If there is one thing everybody who follows world affairs knows about Mikhail Gorbachev, it is that he has become one of the world's most popular leaders. His warm and open political style—whether in small meetings or with massive crowds—and his immense personal charm quickly made him a celebrity as well as a politician. Outside his own country, he is by far the most popular Soviet leader in history. This is especially true in Western Europe, where "Gorby Mania" or "Gorby Fever" took hold as early as his 1984 visit to Great Britain and hit a dizzying peak with Gorbachev's visit to West Germany in 1989. In his first year in office, Gorbachev's popularity rating equaled that of Ronald Reagan, the immensely popular American president from 1981 to 1989.

If Gorbachev's popularity has lagged anywhere, it is at home. There the persistence of hard times and problems has rubbed some of the shine from Gorbachev's image. He is not too impressed with himself and his successes on the world stage to realize this and to understand why. As he commented in a 1987 interview:

> *When people speak of the popularity of Gorbachev they mean not the popularity of a concrete person but a policy which is pursued by the Soviet leadership. . . . If we are consistent in implementing it, both in home and foreign policy, the authority will remain and will increase. If it does not, no style, no personal charm will save us.*[2]

Gorbachev's evaluation of the limits of style and of the need for substance is correct. At the same time, style is very much a part of Gorbachev's policies and reforms. Since his political style—the way in which he relates to the Soviet people—in effect was his first reform, it is important to examine how he likes to live and work.

In some ways Gorbachev is a conventional Soviet leader. He likes to live well. He and Raisa have two Moscow residences, one near the Kremlin and one on

*Gorbachev as world statesman
(counterclockwise from top):
In New York City with President
Reagan and Vice President Bush
in 1988; With British prime
minister Margaret Thatcher in
1984; at the Great Wall of China
with Raisa in 1989; being
greeted by Cuban youngsters
with welcoming signs and flags
during a tour of Havana in 1989.*

the outskirts of the city. (The Soviet Union has no official residence for its leader.) They vacation at luxurious resorts reserved for the country's top leadership. Mikhail dresses well, sometimes in custom-made suits from exclusive London tailors who charge at least $600 per suit. He wears a gold and steel watch estimated to be worth $1,000. Gorbachev's annual salary is about $30,000, or seven times the average Soviet wage. He recently made $600,000 from sales of his book *Perestroika,* but this he donated to the Communist party.

Gorbachev's lifestyle is luxurious by most people's standards, and far beyond what ordinary Soviet citizens enjoy in a country where a pair of durable and comfortable shoes is considered a luxury. But Gorbachev does not overdo it as Brezhnev and his cronies did. Gorbachev may ride in limousines—so do American and European leaders—but he does not have a personal fleet of luxury cars like Brezhnev's (which included a Rolls-Royce, Mercedes, and Cadillac). He shows up at his office at 9 A.M., and often works into the evening. Gorbachev also puts in a six-day week.

In a major break with Soviet tradition, Gorbachev has resisted the flattery and idol worship that has been lavished on previous Soviet leaders. He ordered that no giant poster displays of the sort past leaders loved seeing of themselves be put up in public places. The press has been told not to quote him all the time, and instead quote Marx or Lenin if they must quote somebody. He does not want small events or accomplishments to be inflated into brilliant triumphs that bear no relation to reality. The transcripts of party meetings do not record that his remarks were greeted by "long thunderous applause," as they invariably did under earlier leaders. In short, Gorbachev in power has remained what he always was: a man confident enough to be judged on what he has actually accomplished.

The most dramatic aspect of Gorbachev's political style

is his personal contact with the Soviet people. With the exception of Khrushchev, Soviet leaders have ruled from afar, seldom mingling with the people except in the most formal and stilted settings. This was certainly true during Brezhnev's eighteen years in office. By keeping their distance this way, these leaders had no sense of how the Soviet people lived or felt, and often had little understanding of some of the most important problems in Soviet society. So, when Mikhail Gorbachev became general secretary and immediately went out to speak directly to the Soviet people, he was in a very real sense making an important change in how his country was being governed.

Shortly after becoming general secretary, Gorbachev conducted a tour of Moscow. He made a point of not telling the Moscow party chief about the tour because he wanted to avoid meeting people who had been carefully screened and prepared. He wanted to meet ordinary people who would tell him the truth. As he toured the city's kindergarten schools, supermarkets, and hospitals Gorbachev asked hard questions about shortages, inadequate wages, and poor social services. This pattern has since become the rule. In touring a shipyard in Leningrad, the country's second largest city, Gorbachev cut short the welcoming speech so he could talk with the local workers. It was the same in the countryside. When the general secretary arrived to inspect a farm, he ignored a specially prepared stairway and scrambled down a sharp slope to reach his goal: a potato field. Nor was Gorbachev satisfied to meet only Soviet citizens. While in Washington for his summit meeting with President Reagan in 1987, Gorbachev managed to cause both American and Soviet security men near heart failure by ordering his motorcade to stop and marching into a crowd of onlookers to shake hands and exchange greetings.

A safer way of reaching both the Soviet people and

*The new general secretary chats
with the citizens of Leningrad.*

the citizens of other countries is through the media, especially television. Television in many ways was the enemy of Gorbachev's immediate predecessors. It revealed them in their sickly decline, such as when Chernenko stood before the nation at Andropov's funeral, barely alive himself. Gorbachev is a natural on television. He thinks quickly and is articulate and extremely well informed on all issues. The Gorbachev sense of humor can deflect a pointed question, or soften a blunt answer. His hand gestures, strong and precise, enliven and underscore his words. His eyes flash assurance and confidence, and his smile can be warm and reassuring when he chooses. In an hour-long 1987 interview for the NBC television network, Americans saw a man who was totally comfortable dealing with the give-and-take of a free press, as if he had been doing it all his life.

There is one other essential part of Mikhail Gorbachev's political style: Raisa Maximovna Gorbachev. She is in effect the first Soviet first lady. Khrushchev's and Brezhnev's wives were barely visible. Andropov, supposedly a reformer, kept his wife so far in the background that her existence only became known when she wept over his casket at his funeral. Raisa Gorbachev is not only visible, she is audible. She travels with Mikhail on most of his tours around the country and on his foreign trips. She is not bashful about making her views known on matters from art and fashion to philosophy and politics. Nor are the Gorbachevs shy about their closeness as a couple. One widely reported incident illustrates this. During his 1985 visit to France, Mikhail appeared nervous as he entered the French National Assembly before delivering a major speech. Once he spotted Raisa in the audience, he smiled at her and clearly relaxed. On another occasion Raisa provided the personal touch by looking out for her husband. In 1986 the Gorbachevs were touring the eastern part of the country. While Mikhail was giving an outdoor speech during a rainstorm, Raisa motioned from behind to the official holding an umbrella over her husband that water was running down Mikhail's back. The matter was corrected without him missing a word, and probably without his ever knowing anything was wrong. Raisa has said of their relationship, "I'm very lucky with Mikhail. We are really friends."[3]

Raisa is not without her critics. Her interest in fashion and shopping trips in the West have angered those who feel she is insensitive to what so many lack at home. In private conversation she sometimes is referred to as the "tsarina," a scathing reference to the pre-1917 royal family. At times Raisa has been insensitive. In Washington during the 1987 Gorbachev-Reagan summit Raisa seemed unaware that American First Lady Nancy Reagan had just been through a cancer operation, and the tension between the two women was too visible to be covered up by public relations announcements.

Raisa Gorbachev also can be very dogmatic. She is a convinced and sometimes inflexible Marxist. Her doctoral dissertation reveals both her intellectual strengths and her dogmatism. In that work she deplored the lack of basic comforts, such as central heating and running water, available to the peasants. She focused on the illiteracy among older people, and the burdens, including heavy physical labor, of rural women. Yet as a Marxist and atheist she was annoyed that the rural people still celebrate religious holidays and that they play dominoes, which she considered a waste of time.

Part of the criticism against Raisa Gorbachev goes beyond her personality to the process of change, of which she is a symbol. Raisa has been rebuked for being too forward for a proper Soviet woman. There are rumors that she influences her husband on policy matters, which bothers many people who adhere to traditional attitudes that are still widely held in the Soviet Union. While most women work outside the home, the prestigious jobs are

*Raisa Gorbachev and Nancy Reagan pose
for photographers during the 1987 summit
meeting held in Washington, D.C.*

largely held by the men. Many women are members of the Communist party, but they become increasingly scarce at the top of the party ladder. Since the founding of the Soviet Union, only one woman has ever been a full member of the Politburo, and that was in Khrushchev's time. Gorbachev did promote a woman, Alexandra Biryukova, to the Secretariat in 1986 and then to candidate status on the Politburo in 1988.

Conveniences that Western women take for granted, from home appliances to products for feminine hygiene needs, simply are not available in the Soviet Union. One of the worst inadequacies of the Soviet health care system is its neglect of women's needs. Because it is so difficult to get contraceptives, the Soviet abortion rate is one of the highest in the world, close to four times that in the United States. One Western observer has accurately summarized the Soviet woman's lot:

> *The combination of work, domestic chores, the difficulty of shopping and the problems of arranging childcare means that the average Soviet woman spends her life rushing. She gets up early to prepare breakfast, takes her child to the day-care center, goes to work, shops in her lunch hour and even in work hours, travels back to pick up her child, to prepare an evening meal, to clean up the flat [apartment]. The public transport systems are more crowded, the gaps between stations longer, the food supplies in the shops more problematic, the vacuum cleaners less efficient, the refrigerators smaller, the freezers rare, and the convenience foods even rarer.[4]*

It is against this background of tradition and neglect that Raisa's public activities offend conservative Soviet citizens. This does not seem to bother or intimidate her at all. She enjoys her husband's support as a public figure, something that Mikhail has made clear in statements to the press. Although he occasionally has become annoyed when questioned by Western reporters about Raisa's activities, it is characteristic of Gorbachev to also use humor to stand up for his wife. When asked during a 1989 visit to Leningrad why his wife was not with him, Gorbachev wryly observed he wanted to demonstrate he could govern without Raisa at his side. Raisa is more direct. She insists her critics are men. "But the women are all for me," she stresses. Raisa once even called over a foreign reporter to witness the following exchange between herself and several women deputies to the new Supreme Soviet:

> *"All women are for you," one exclaimed.*
> *"Write this down," the first lady [Raisa] instructed the press.*
> *"That's right," chimed in another. "That's exactly how the spouse, the wife of the General Secretary should be, like Raisa Maximovna, with her intellect and her schooling, with her charm. And we're proud of her."*
> *"We finally have someone to show off abroad," the chorus continued. "At last! At last! Someone to show off."*
> *"Write that down, if you're not ashamed," Mrs. Gorbachev repeated, glowing with triumph. "I always knew the women were with me."*[5]

Raisa Gorbachev had managed her own career for many years. She began as a teacher in Stavropol. In 1978, when Mikhail was called to Moscow, she began teaching Marxist philosophy at Moscow State University. She gave up this post and her career in 1985 when Mikhail was elected general secretary. But Raisa did not slip into her husband's shadow. She played a major role in the creation of the Soviet Cultural Fund, an organization dedicated to involving young people in the arts. Raisa continues to define the role that many Soviet females proudly call the "new Soviet woman." She also undoubtedly will continue to influence her husband on issues of the day, not only those relating to Soviet women, but those concerning all people in the Soviet Union and, for that matter, people everywhere.

Political style, as Gorbachev has observed, means nothing without substance, and Gorbachev came into office determined to make substantial change. Gorbachev's overall strategy, which has evolved over time, is complex and involves many interrelated programs. It can be summarized, however, by four terms. The first is *perestroika,* or "restructuring." *Perestroika* assumes that the Soviet economy will have to be overhauled if it is to be modern and efficient enough to maintain the Soviet Union as a superpower. This will not be easy. Change will involve sacrifice on the part of people who already have many complaints about their economic conditions. No matter, says Gorbachev, because the Soviet Union has no choice.

> *Perestroika is an urgent necessity. . . . This society is ripe for change. It has long been yearning for it. Any delay in beginning perestroika could have led to an exacerbated internal situation in the near future, which, to put it bluntly, would have been fraught with serious social, economic, and political crises.*[6]

Closely related to perestroika, and essential to it, is *glasnost,* or "openness." *Glasnost* involves a drastic reduction of censorship in art, literature, news reporting, and the like. This must be done for several reasons. First, the Soviet Union's educated elite cannot work effectively to solve the nation's problems unless it has access to a wide range of ideas, both at home and abroad. Second, it is impossible to solve a problem unless one understands it fully. Prior to Gorbachev, secrecy was the rule, in part to keep information from the West and in part to maintain the myth at home that all was well in Soviet life. This led to a number of absurdities. For example, until recently, many Soviet officials actually relied on foreign data about their society in their work, since so little reliable information was available at home. Gorbachev has made it clear that without glasnost it will be impossible to get very much done:

> *The new atmosphere is, perhaps, most vividly manifest in glasnost. We want more openness . . . in every sphere of life. People should know what is good, and what is bad, too, in order to multiply the good and to combat the bad. . . . Truth is the main thing. Lenin said: more light! Let the party know everything. As never before we need no dark corners where mold can reappear. . . .*[7]

Another key element is a word few people associate with the Soviet Union: *demokratizatsia,* or "democratization." This does *not* mean democracy as Americans understand the term, at least not to Gorbachev and other Soviet leaders. Until 1990 Gorbachev flatly opposed a multi-party state where the Communist party could be voted out of office. To him, demokratizatsia now meant that some choice would come into the system—that in factories, in elections to government bodies, and possibly even in party elections there might be a choice of candidates. The hope was that *glasnost* and demokratizatsia, even in their limited Soviet style, would entice ordinary citizens to pitch in voluntarily to help the reform effort. This participation was essential because unless Gorbachev had genuine popular support and help it would be impossible to overhaul the economy and bring it up to foreign standards.

103

Finally there is *novoe myshlenie,* or "new thinking." Although there is new thinking in every aspect of Gorbachev's program, this term refers most specifically to the Soviet Union's relationship with the West, which has for so long been marked by hostility. Ever since the Bolsheviks seized power in 1917, the Soviets have officially been committed to overthrowing the capitalist system. Many observers believe that in fact the Soviet Union gave up that dream a long time ago. Still, Soviet expansionism after World War II was the key factor in the arms race and tension known as the Cold War that has dominated the international scene for over forty years. The trouble for Gorbachev is that military spending is one of the heaviest anchors dragging down the Soviet economy. He needs the resources currently going into arms to rebuild his country's civilian economy. This helps to account for the various arms control initiatives that have flowed like a steady stream from the Kremlin since 1985. At the same time, Gorbachev has made it clear that there are more important issues that all countries must now deal with, perhaps first among them being the environment.

Despite the emergence of these grand goals over time, Gorbachev's first year in office was one of small steps and hints of more to come, probably because Gorbachev did not appreciate the scope of the problems before him. The larger and bolder steps were to come later, as Gorbachev seems to have concluded that more radical measures were necessary. Also, before he could take any bold steps Gorbachev had to counter the considerable oppo-

Glasnost *at work: Moscow citizens attend a photo exhibit honoring the memory of victims of Joseph Stalin's repression.*

sition to reform by consolidating his hold on power. *Perestroika* inevitably meant that thousands of officials would have to be fired throughout the party and state bureaucracies. Many of these people were in influential positions. In addition, the reformers themselves were divided. Some wanted to push ahead full steam, while others were concerned that reform could run out of control and lead to trouble. So Gorbachev was restrained not only by the difficulty of the job at hand, but also by powerful political forces pitted against him.

The year 1985 did see a few minor economic reforms. A few factories were allowed to keep their profits, instead of turning them over to the state, and to use them to finance their own development. In agriculture, Gorbachev combined six ministries into one superministry. The effect of this, as might be suspected, was to tighten the deadening grip of the Moscow planners on the farms, rather than reducing it. Some incompetent administrators were fired and an attempt was made to tighten up discipline among the workers. In cultural life, there was the first glimmer of *glasnost* in the form of a major prose/poem about Soviet history by Yevgeny Yevtushenko and two plays about current corruption in the party.

Gorbachev's most visible policy at home was his attempt to slay what the Russians call the "green snake"—alcoholism. He closed down two-thirds of the liquor stores and cut the hours of those that remained. The fine for public drunkenness was increased tenfold. During the 1986 New Year's celebrations, for the first time in memory there were no alcoholic beverages for sale on Moscow's streets; they were replaced by soft drinks. For his efforts, General Secretary Gorbachev was nicknamed the "mineral water secretary." To what extent this reflected resentment or admiration is an open question.

What is beyond question is that the "green snake" refused to die. Not even the supposedly voluntary All-Union Voluntary Society for the Battle for Sobriety, which by 1987 grew to 14 million members, could make a difference. The public did not always respond the way Gorbachev hoped. Heavy drinking is deeply rooted in Russian culture. To get around Gorbachev's restrictions there was a dramatic increase in home brewing of alcoholic beverages. This type of resistance eventually forced a reversal of several of Gorbachev's policies, beginning as early as the end of 1986.

Meanwhile, Gorbachev worked to lessen tensions with the Soviet Union's neighbors. Although concrete actions were yet to come, Gorbachev had soothing words for everybody. He informed the nations of Western Europe that they and the Soviet Union shared what he called "our common house." To his neighbors to the east, especially Japan and the People's Republic of China, Gorbachev stressed "our common Asiatic heritage." To all the nations of the world Gorbachev announced in August 1985 that the Soviet Union was stopping all nuclear tests, which it did for about eighteen months.

This step was directed primarily at the United States—still the Soviet Union's most important concern abroad. During 1985 the two countries began to improve their strained relations. Arms control talks resumed, as did some cultural exchanges that had been stopped by the United States after the Soviet invasion of Afghanistan. The highlight of the year was the Gorbachev/Reagan summit meeting in November in Geneva. No serious business was conducted at that meeting. The intent was to have the two leaders get to know each other and to set the stage for progress later on. This "Fireside Summit" (the two leaders held one of their conversations in front of a roaring fire in a small hut near Lake Geneva) did not always go well. The two men disagreed about a wide range of issues. As Gorbachev put it, "our discussions were frank, long, sharp, and, at times, very sharp." But both leaders were determined to make a fresh start in Soviet-American relations. They therefore used what

Gorbachev called their "springboard" toward better relations, "the realization that a nuclear war cannot be won and must never be fought."[8] The result was the following scene, just after the two men had disagreed strongly about Reagan's program to build a space-based defense against nuclear missiles, the "Strategic Defense Initiative" or "Star Wars" plan:

> *This time it was Gorbachev who bridged the gap. "We must continue talking about it," he said. Reagan agreed. On the return from the small hut to the villa, he said, "I want to invite you to come and visit me in the United States next year." "And I want to invite you to come to the Soviet Union." "I accept," said Reagan; "I accept," Gorbachev echoed. They shook hands with a smile, and the mood lifted.[9]*

Gorbachev's most concrete gain during 1985 was in the political arena back home. He succeeded in pushing aside the remaining members of the Brezhnev generation. Eighty-three-year-old Prime Minister Nikolai Tikhonov gave way to Nikolai Ryzhkov, an experienced and competent manager and economics expert. Foreign Minister Andrei Gromyko was kicked upstairs to the largely ceremonial post of president of the Soviet Union. He was replaced by Gorbachev's friend Eduard Shevardnadze. The pattern extended to other important government posts as well as to key party positions. By the end of the year Gorbachev had a working majority on the Politburo.

But this majority included men who could and did disagree with him. The most important of them was Yegor Ligachev. Like Gorbachev, Ligachev was a protégé of Yuri Andropov. He emerged as the party's number-two man, and was clearly more conservative and cautious than Gorbachev. Ligachev was quite prepared to oppose the general secretary when he saw fit. One member of the new leadership closer to Ligachev than to Gorbachev was Viktor Chebrikov, the head of the KGB. Gorbachev's closest ally on the Politburo was Shevardnadze. Another close associate was Alexander Yakovlev. The former Soviet ambassador to Canada, Yakovlev is totally committed to *perestroika* and has clearly influenced Gorbachev towards more radical reform. But Yakovlev only became a candidate Politburo member in 1987.

The year 1986 began with a major event, the Twenty-seventh Congress of the Communist party. It was yet another example of Gorbachev's luck blending with his skill. Party congresses take place every five years, and this one, occurring only one year after Gorbachev took office, gave him a chance to do some more housecleaning. He chose the precise opening date, and it was a significant one. February 25, 1986, was thirty years to the day after the opening of Khrushchev's Twentieth Congress, the Congress of de-Stalinization and reform.

The Twenty-seventh Congress was the most open congress since the rise of Stalin in the 1920s. There was actually open debate and disagreement, something the party had not seen in almost sixty years. Gorbachev himself made it clear where he stood. The term "radical reform" appeared repeatedly in his report to the congress. There was no doubt of the job at hand or the urgency it demanded:

> Today, the prime task of the Party and the entire people is to reverse resolutely the unfavorable tendencies in the development of the economy, to impart to it . . . dynamism and to give scope to the initiative and creativity of the masses, to truly revolutionary change.[10]

The congress enabled Gorbachev to introduce a new party program and increase the number of his supporters on the Central Committee and Politburo. It adopted rules that made it easier to move against corruption. But Gorbachev did not always get his way. A majority of the Central Committee remained holdovers from the Brezhnev era. For instance, a rule Gorbachev wanted that would have made it easier to replace party officials was not adopted. Practical plans for economic reform remained modest rather than radical. In short, while Gorbachev emerged from the congress stronger than ever, it was clear that there was significant opposition to his reform program.

Shortly after the congress closed, another problem literally exploded in Gorbachev's face. On April 25, 1986, the peaceful spring air of the Ukraine was shattered by thundering noise, roaring flame, and searing heat. What must have seemed like the devil's fiery work was in reality the poorly executed atomic work of man. An explosion had destroyed one of the reactors at the Chernobyl nuclear power plant, sending unprecedented and disastrous amounts of radioactive poisons shooting upward and outward across the countryside.

The Chernobyl disaster recalled the 1958 Soviet nuclear disaster in the Ural Mountains, when a nuclear waste dump exploded and turned a small region into a wasteland. Chernobyl, however, was far worse. This time air currents carried the nuclear poisons thousands of miles across the Soviet countryside and into Central and Western Europe. The political fallout for Gorbachev and *glasnost* was also serious. The government, and Gorbachev, fell silent. No announcement of the disaster came until radiation was detected in Western Europe. It took three days for an official response. Fifteen more days passed before Gorbachev, supposedly the apostle of openness, finally spoke.

When he did, it was his worst performance to date. It is true there had been exaggerated reports of the disaster in the Western press. But this was largely because

The Gorbachevs and their aides wear white gowns during a visit to a control room at the ill-fated Chernobyl nuclear plant.

of the Soviet Union's failure to report the facts. Gorbachev seized on these reports to attack both the Western press and its politicians. He angrily denounced "a veritable mountain of lies, most dishonest and malicious lies" that he said appeared in the Western press. He also accused certain Western politicians of trying to "defame the Soviet Union."[11] His anger was deeply felt. A year after the explosion, Gorbachev wrote in his book *Perestroika* how people from abroad had come to the Soviet Union's aid, and how he "appreciated the understanding and help of all those who felt for us in our misfortune. . . ." Yet in the very same sentence Gorbachev complained about how his country had "witnessed again how much malice and malevolence there was in the world."[12]

In fact, the Soviet government was painfully slow to respond to the crisis. Only heroic actions by local firefighters, several of whom died of radiation sickness, prevented a greater disaster. Meanwhile Moscow delayed evacuation of the civilian population from the area around the smoldering reactor. Thirty-six hours after the explosion, children were playing in the streets in the village of Pripat, only 5 miles (8 km) from the reactor. It took a full week to evacuate the larger town of Chernobyl a little farther away.

Over the next weeks and months the Soviets soon recovered by embarking on an efficient cleanup operation. The government issued a long and comprehensive report on the disaster. Yet nothing could prevent the billions of dollars in damage caused by the accident to water, crops, and farm animals, not only in the Soviet Union but in many Western European countries. The immediate death toll was held to thirty-one, mainly those who were at the reactor when it exploded and those brought in to contain the fire immediately thereafter. The number of long-term deaths from radiation poisoning, of course, is unknown, although they probably will be measured in the thousands, and possibly tens of thousands. Also unknown are the environmental effects on the Ukraine, the Soviet Union's breadbasket.

Another unknown is Chernobyl's effect on Gorbachev. The disaster has not led him to stop the Soviet Union's development of nuclear power to generate electricity—plans remain to build new plants. It did, however, seem to have convinced him that change had to come faster, including more openness or *glasnost*. It may well have heightened his overall concerns about the nuclear threat to the world. In *Perestroika*, published in 1987, he noted that Chernobyl "taught us a grave lesson in what an atom out of control is capable of doing, even an atom used for peaceful purposes."[13] And it seems to have affected Gorbachev's outlook on the environment in general, convincing him of how fragile and vulnerable it really is.

The Chernobyl incident did not stop Mikhail Gorbachev. Rather, during the next several years his intensified efforts at reform pushed him to the very center of the world political stage.

7
PRESIDENT AND
WORLD STATESMAN

In the months that followed, Gorbachev turned from problems caused by the peaceful use of the atom to the threat of its possible use in wartime. By mid-1986 he made a forceful but totally unrealistic call for nuclear disarmament by the year 2000. Whether or not he was serious, most of the West's political leaders, including President Ronald Reagan, considered it just another example of Soviet propaganda. During the summer of 1986, Soviet-American relations chilled. The United States arrested Gennady Zakharov, a Soviet official who worked at the United Nations, for trying to buy American secrets from an FBI undercover agent. The Soviets retaliated by arresting Nicholas Daniloff, an American journalist. They accused him of spying, a charge that few believed. In a fashion typical of international diplomacy, the two sides arranged an exchange of their respective prisoners, without admitting that this in fact was what had taken place.

However, both Reagan and Gorbachev wanted to meet again to work toward nuclear arms control. Gorbachev suggested the meeting be held in Reykjavik, the capital of Iceland. This tiny island nation in the North Atlantic lies about midway between Moscow and Washington. Perhaps Gorbachev thought it was a suitable place for bridging differences between the superpowers. Whatever the reasons, hopes for a dramatic breakthrough in arms control soared in many world capitals.

Excitement mounted once the two leaders arrived in Reykjavik in October 1986. As usual, Raisa accompanied her husband, although Nancy Reagan stayed home. No sooner had they arrived when it quickly became clear to Gorbachev and Reagan that they were in trouble. Gorbachev came prepared to make some significant concessions, but only if the United States would abandon Reagan's Star Wars [SDI] program. This the American president was unwilling to do. One of Reagan's comments after the first negotiating session summed up both the potential and the problem of the Reykjavik summit: "He's brought a whole lot of proposals, but I'm afraid he's going after SDI."[1]

Reagan was correct about what Gorbachev wanted. He also was justified in worrying about how SDI would affect the negotiations. SDI proved to be the iceberg that sank the Reykjavik summit. It was a bitter disappointment to both sides. Both leaders had felt they were close to an agreement for huge cuts in nuclear weapons, cuts that held the promise of ending the arms race. After negotiations broke down, Gorbachev did not hide his own frustration. In a prepared statement, he told a news conference: "Regrettably, the Americans came to this meeting empty-handed, with the same old moth-eaten trash from which the Geneva talks are already choking." At the same time, echoing President Reagan's post-summit comments, he tried to be optimistic about the future:

> *I think, nevertheless, that the entire meeting here was of major significance. We did, after all, come close to reaching agreements. . . . The very path that we have traversed in reaching these agreements here in Iceland on major cuts in nuclear*

*Both leaders' faces
show their disappointment
as they conclude their
1986 summit meeting
in Reykjavik, Iceland,
when both sides failed
to reach an agreement
on arms control.*

weapons has given us substantial experience and we have made considerable gains.[2]

Gorbachev's brave front could not cover the failure of the summit. Reykjavik was the most unsuccessful Soviet-American summit meeting in twenty-five years. The silent, grim expressions on the two leaders' faces when they said good-bye to each other told more than any of their words. But the failure seems only to have led both leaders to persist. At stake for Ronald Reagan, nearing the last quarter of his presidency, was a place in history as a peacemaker. For Mikhail Gorbachev, just beginning his years as general secretary, ending the arms race was essential. Only then could he spend less on the military and use those savings to rebuild the Soviet economy.

It took more than a year to cross that bridge again. Meanwhile, Gorbachev inched his way across it by talking softly to his next-door neighbors, America's allies in Europe. To those nations, living since the end of World War II in fear that the huge Soviet Red Army would one day roll westward, Gorbachev said, "In the European building, every apartment is entitled to protect itself against burglars, but only in such a way as not to demolish the next-door apartment."[3]

By December 1987 the two leaders were together again, this time in Washington. It was Gorbachev's first visit to the United States and he spent four hectic days in Washington. In this third Reagan-Gorbachev summit in less than three years, the superpowers were more modest in their goals. Instead of discussing their largest and most powerful long-range nuclear weapons, or "strategic" weapons, they focused on smaller intermediate-range weapons. These weapons were based in Europe, those in the West aimed at the Soviet Union, and those in the East aimed at the countries of the NATO alliance. In addition, this time, unlike at Reykjavik where

117

real negotiations took place, the necessary agreements had already been worked out.

Gorbachev was warmly greeted at the White House by President Reagan, the same man who only a few years earlier had called the Soviet Union an "evil empire." This time Reagan told Gorbachev that, "I have always felt that our people should have been better friends long ago."[4] Gorbachev's remarks went further. He told the American president that they both had even broader responsibilities:

> *History has charged the governments of our countries, and the two of us, Mr. President, with the solemn duty to justify the hopes of Americans and Soviet people, and the people of the world over, to undo the logic of the arms race by working together in good faith.*[5]

And work Gorbachev did. His meetings with Reagan were only a part of his busy schedule. He met American artists, scientists, and intellectuals at the Soviet embassy. He spoke with leaders of the United States Congress. American media executives and businessmen spoke with Gorbachev at two other meetings. Gorbachev gave a speech to both the American and Soviet people, and also found time to hold a news conference.

This grinding pace took its toll. Gorbachev lost his temper several times, including once when he spoke harshly to President Reagan about the issue of human rights. But the human rights issue refused to go away. Several groups of protesters stalked the general secretary as he went from meeting to meeting. Among them were advocates for various minority national groups in the Soviet Union who have suffered discrimination. These included Soviet Jews seeking the right to emigrate, and supporters of Latvian, Lithuanian, and Estonian independence. Perhaps the angriest group of demonstrators were those protesting the Soviet war in Afghanistan. Their shouts included "Death to Gorbachev." If this all bothered the general secretary, it did not intimidate him. While riding in a motorcade with Vice-President George Bush, Gorbachev ordered his car stopped. He quickly stepped out, and before his security guards could do anything about it, marched up to the crowd standing at the curb and began to shake hands. No American politician could have done it better.

The treaty signed in Washington—known as the Intermediate Forces or INF treaty—required both sides to eliminate all their intermediate-range nuclear missiles. That in itself did not radically change the number of nuclear weapons in the world. Only about 4 percent of the superpowers' weapons were in that category. But for the first time in the history of the arms race, an entire class of nuclear weapons was eliminated. The Soviets also agreed to strict inspection requirements to insure the treaty's terms were carried out. The treaty was a major triumph for both men, and enabled Gorbachev to go home better able to deal with his critics in the party leadership. But as Gorbachev observed at his White House farewell ceremony, the INF treaty was only a small first step:

> *Today the Soviet Union and the United States are closer to the common goals of strengthening international security. But this goal has not yet been reached. There is still much work to be done, and we must get down to it without delay.*[6]

Gorbachev did not delay. One of the worst foreign relations problems he inherited was the Soviet involvement in Afghanistan. By the end of 1987 the Soviet effort to prop up the local Communist government there against anti-Communist guerrillas was stalemated. Over 100,000 Soviet soldiers were struggling in a war increasingly expensive in terms of both human lives and money. In February 1988, Gorbachev announced that all Soviet troops would be withdrawn from Afghanistan by early 1989. On February 15, 1989, the last of the Soviet soldiers, a general, left Afghanistan. He walked across a small bridge at the Soviet-Afghan border, hugged his son, who greeted him with a bouquet of carnations, and did not look back. "There is not a single Soviet soldier left behind me," the general commented. "Our nine-year stay ends with this."[7]

That "stay" had cost the lives of 15,000 Soviets and hundreds of thousands of Afghans. Millions of Afghans had become refugees. Thousands of surviving Soviet soldiers were maimed or addicted to drugs. In effect the Red Army, the proud victor over Hitler's ultra-modern legions in World War II, had been beaten by a collection of ragtag, poorly armed guerrilla bands. But at least the war was over. Mikhail Gorbachev had closed what he once called his country's "open wound."

Even as the last Soviet troops were moving northward to the Soviet border, Gorbachev was working to improve his country's image elsewhere. One factor that has fueled the Soviet-American arms race for over forty years is each side's fear of the type of new arms the other might build. Under Brezhnev during the 1960s and 1970s, the Soviet Union engaged in the greatest arms

The USSR's "open wound": Gorbachev closed a painful chapter in Soviet history when he authorized the withdrawal of Soviet troops from Afghanistan. Here, soldiers in Soviet tanks are coming home from the front.

buildup in history. Its official goal was to give the Soviet Union absolute security. But the plan backfired, leading instead to the American arms buildup of the 1980s. It also made many of the Soviet Union's neighbors fearful, from Western Europe to China and Japan. Now Gorbachev began to talk about a change in approach. He said that the time of building more and more arms was past; it made more sense, Gorbachev added, to reach the level of "reasonable sufficiency." This meant having enough arms to deter any potential attacker, but not to build new weapons just because the other side was doing so.

Many people were skeptical, in part because there were no concrete actions backing up Gorbachev's words. To convince the doubters, in December 1988 Gorbachev came to the United Nations headquarters in New York. Not since Nikita Khrushchev, almost thirty years earlier, had a Soviet leader spoken to the world from the podium of the UN General Assembly.

Gorbachev's theme was clear. Modern technology had created a world in which no nation could be secure at the expense of others. All nations now lived in an interdependent world in which cooperation was essential for survival. The time had come for all nations to rethink their foreign policies:

> *It is obvious, for instance, that the use or threat of force no longer can or must be an instrument of foreign policy. This applies above all to nuclear arms, but that is not the only thing that matters. All of us, and primarily the stronger of us, must exercise self-restraint and totally rule out any outward-oriented use of force.*[8]

These were fine words, but how was the Soviet Union going to back them up? Gorbachev delivered a blockbuster: the Soviet Union would cut its armed forces by

500,000 men, about 10 percent of its total troops, and by 10,000 tanks. These cuts would be "unilateral," that is, the Soviets would make them without waiting for the United States to do the same. There was, of course, skepticism, and with good reason. What type of units would be dismantled, poorly equipped ones or modern ones capable of launching lightning attacks in Europe? Although this and similar questions remained unanswered, it was indisputable that Gorbachev had scored a public relations success. Once again he had made himself the international man of the hour.

Afterwards, Gorbachev undertook the even more difficult challenge of taking his act to the streets of New York City. Once again he was a success. A *New York Times* headline announced the existence of a "Gorbachev Spell." It was clear that Gorbachev was doing wonders for his nation's image, which in the West for years had been of a big, menacing Russian bear. As the *Times* reported:

> *It is one thing to arm a nation against an impersonal Soviet threat. It is another to worry about a man who bedevils his K.G.B. security guards by jumping out of his car at 50th Street and Broadway and raises his hands in a "Rocky" salute in the glare of a Coca-Cola sign and whose wife spends a happy afternoon trying creams and perfumes in a Fifth Avenue salon.*[9]

Not everything went well while Gorbachev was in New York. On December 8, a devastating earthquake shattered the southern Soviet republic of Armenia. The death toll quickly passed 50,000; 500,000 were left homeless. A shaken Gorbachev immediately cut short his New York visit to return home and visit the disaster area. As usual, Raisa was at his side.

A huge spontaneous outpouring of foreign help for

*Gorbachev addresses the people in Leninakan, a
city severely damaged by the Armenian earthquake.*

the quake victims set an example for international cooperation across political lines. Aid poured in from the United States, Great Britain, Japan, Argentina, France, and many other countries. Israel, a country with whom the Soviet Union refuses to have diplomatic relations, sent a team specially trained for rescuing people from collapsed buildings. But no amount of help could change a reality of entire cities destroyed and hundreds of thousands of lives shattered. Nor could it hide the inefficiency of the Soviet relief effort, the same inefficiency that plagued other areas of Soviet life. Three days after the quake, a Soviet relief airplane crashed, killing seventy-eight people. Even a half year after the quake, local residents were angry and frustrated at the slow pace of reconstruction. Inevitably, much of this resentment was directed at the man with final responsibility for what goes on in the Soviet Union, Mikhail Gorbachev.

Despite the Armenian tragedy, Gorbachev in the late 1980s proved skilled in increasing his political strength at home. The turnover of important personnel in the party and government continued. By the spring of 1988, 40 percent of the Central Committee, 60 percent of the regional party first secretaries, and 70 percent of the government ministers had been replaced. Eight of the fourteen Politburo members were new. Of course, not all of these new people were totally committed Gorbachev supporters. Strong differences of opinion were obvious among the top party leaders, with Yegor Ligachev increasingly emerging as opposed to both the scope and pace of reform. Still, these changes strengthened Gorbachev considerably.

Several dramatic events signaled Gorbachev's growing power. In June 1987 the Central Committee adopted a broad economic reform program that Gorbachev advocated. It called for Soviet factories to be freed from the control of central planners in Moscow. Since 1929, those planners had controlled the country's factories, dictating prices, wages, and most other critical aspects of factory operation. Beginning in 1988, these controls would be eliminated for many factories. By 1991, all production would be freed of them. In short, the marketplace would replace central planners in determining a large part of what is produced. The goal was to increase efficiency. However, it was also true that these reforms would mean unemployment, first for many central planners who were no longer needed, and then for many workers whose factories were unable to compete in the marketplace.

Getting his economic program in place did not mean it would work. Gorbachev's road at times was a bumpy one. One jolt occurred in October 1987 when Boris Yeltsin, considered a Gorbachev supporter, attacked the general secretary for moving too slowly with *perestroika*. Yeltsin leveled most of his criticism at Yegor Ligachev, Gorbachev's main rival on the Politburo. Ligachev was emerging as the most powerful critic of Gorbachev's program. But because of the harshness of Yeltsin's attack, Gorbachev was forced to break with him. Yeltsin was removed from the Politburo and from his post as the party leader in Moscow. While this obviously made Yeltsin the big loser, Gorbachev and his program also were bruised by the Yeltsin affair.

A second jolt occurred in March 1988, while Gorbachev was away on a foreign visit. A leading Soviet magazine published a letter written by a chemistry teacher named Nina Andreeva. The "Andreeva letter" was inspired by Ligachev and others opposed to the direction of Gorbachev's reforms. The letter attacked Gorbachev by endorsing much of the Stalinist past that Gorbachev was trying to undo. One of Andreeva's techniques, sadly familiar to anyone who has studied Russian and Soviet history, was to use open and vicious anti-Semitic slogans to attack her opponents. But what was probably most disturbing was that in Gorbachev's absence, nothing was done to answer the letter. With their leader absent, the advocates of *perestroika* and *glasnost* were frozen in fear.

The situation resembled the atmosphere during the summer of 1987, when Gorbachev had disappeared from public view for fifty-two days. Rumors spread, and of course, Gorbachev resurfaced. It turned out he had been on vacation and working on his book *Perestroika,* which he had finally finished. In the 1988 situation, Gorbachev returned again, but he was silent about the "Andreeva letter." Three long weeks after its appearance he launched a vigorous counterattack. Although Ligachev was forced to retreat, the point was made that Gorbachev still faced strong opposition.

Gorbachev's offensive continued as the year wore on. The setting was the Nineteenth Party Conference. Party conferences are second only to party congresses in importance, although none had been called since 1941. Gorbachev wanted one in order to push his political changes. When he got it late in June of 1988, he made the most of his new opportunity.

Oddly enough, while Gorbachev was the most powerful man at the conference, the most visible sparks of its stormy meetings were generated by others. They flashed when Boris Yeltsin and Yegor Ligachev openly attacked each other.

The real business of the conference, however, concerned the structure of the Soviet government. Gorbachev wanted it overhauled. His goal was to strengthen the government and give it some real power. This would make it more difficult for the party, where opposition to reform remained strong, to block changes that Gorbachev wanted.

Gorbachev got his way. The party conference voted to abolish the old parliament, called the Supreme Soviet. It would be replaced by a 2,250-member "Congress of People's Deputies." Elections to this body would be conducted in a radical new way: there would be a choice of candidates! The old system of elections, dating back to Lenin's time, in which there was only one party-approved candidate for each post, was to be abolished.

Once elected by the population at large, the Congress of People's Deputies would elect a president, the president of the Soviet Union. He would have far more power than the current Soviet president, whose post was only ceremonial. The Congress of People's Deputies would also elect a smaller body, called the Supreme Soviet, which would have about 500 members and conduct the day-to-day business of the country. If actually put into practice, the resolutions of this conference promised political changes of historic importance.

One other thing was new about the Nineteenth Party Conference—the extent and openness of the debate. The conference was broadcast on Soviet television for all to see. As Gorbachev put it in his closing speech:

> *The Palace of Congresses [where these meetings take place] has not known such discussions, comrades, and, I think, we will not err from the truth by saying that nothing of the kind has occurred in the country for nearly six decades.*[10]

In October Gorbachev pressed his advantage at a Central Committee meeting. Here Gorbachev pushed aside Andrei Gromyko, the last powerful member of the Brezhnev generation. Gromyko's post of Soviet president went to Gorbachev. Although it was only a ceremonial post (the government had not yet been reorganized according to the resolutions of the party conference) it increased Gorbachev's prestige. More important, he was able to arrange a shift in responsibilities that weakened Ligachev's position. Ligachev was given responsibility for agriculture, the thankless job Gorbachev had held prior to 1985. Another noteworthy development was Alexandra Biryukova's promotion to the Politburo.

Although she was only a candidate member, she was the first woman to sit on that body in any capacity since 1961, and only the second woman since the Bolshevik Revolution of 1917.

Gorbachev consolidated his power further during 1989. Once again, he demonstrated his boldness by traveling a rough and uncharted road. In March the elections to the Congress of People's Deputies took place as promised. And as promised, many of the seats were contested, often by candidates who did not belong to the Communist party. It was a rough-and-tumble campaign, the first reasonably free political election in the Soviet Union since 1917 (an election Lenin and the Bolsheviks decisively lost). An unheard-of event—televised debates between candidates—became common.

There is little doubt that the Soviet people enjoyed this strange, new experience. And there is no doubt they took it seriously. The results were a shock. In the past, Soviet citizens routinely went to the polls to vote for the one party candidate, who inevitably received 99 percent of the vote. This time party candidates won a majority of the seats, but they also lost about 20 percent of the seats. Some candidates even lost when they had no opponent! This occurred because they failed to get the required 50 percent of the vote. Among the losers were the head of the Leningrad party organization, the mayor of Moscow, and the mayor of Kiev, the capital of the Ukraine. Nor were all the party members who won strict followers of the party line. Boris Yeltsin, demoted and rejected by his party, although still a party member, stunned everyone by winning 89 percent of the vote in his Moscow district.

What did Gorbachev think about all this? He hailed what he called the "people's power" that had emerged in the election. He pointed out to his conservative opponents that the election demonstrated that the desire for change was widespread among the Soviet people.

He added that the party's losses were a part of the evolving democratic process he supported and assured the party there was no cause for concern. Still, although the election on balance strengthened Gorbachev, it must have increased the feeling among conservative circles that reform was going too fast and could lurch out of control. Gorbachev knew this, and privately it must have worried him. In public, however, he had this to say:

> *Some have already gone so far as to say that, in a manner of speaking, both democracy and glasnost are very nearly a disaster. And the fact that the people have begun to act, that they no longer wish to remain silent and insist on their demand, is perceived as a defect of perestroika. I for one, comrades, see this as a success of perestroika.*[11]

To ensure that success, Gorbachev quickly moved once again against his opponents in the party. Ever since he came to power, his support had been weakest in the Central Committee, where many old holdovers from the Brezhnev years still sat. In April 1989, Gorbachev engineered the removal of 110 of those members, seventy-four of whom were full, voting members. In their place he promoted twenty-four supporters to full, voting membership. Among those Gorbachev now pushed into retirement was Gromyko, a major political figure for over thirty years. (He died a few months later at the age of seventy-nine.) Aside from the old Brezhnev generation, another loser in Gorbachev's latest shuffle was the military. Its Central Committee representation declined by almost 40 percent, which was very important, considering Gorbachev's stated desire to reduce military spending.

The following month the newly elected Congress of People's Deputies met for the first time. Aside from being a major political event, this meeting was the largest media hit in Soviet history. It was covered live on television across the Soviet Union's twelve time zones and watched by no less than 200 million people, more than 70 percent of the country's population. Gorbachev soon found out that the deputies took their new positions seriously—both as representatives of the people and as celebrities of a sort. At the meeting there was plenty of dissent and anger, perhaps more than Gorbachev might have wanted. For example, the scientist Andrei Sakharov warned against Gorbachev accumulating too much power. A former Olympic star lashed out at the KGB in no uncertain terms, saying "The KGB is not just a service, it's a real underground empire that hasn't divulged its secrets yet—except for some excavated graves."[12]

Most deputies, of course, simply echoed the line of the leadership. But even they represented something new, as hundreds of them marched to the podium to have their say before the nation. As one Soviet media official observed in amazement:

> Something is really turning over in our national consciousness. The deputies are realizing the people are watching them, the voters can see them live, and the level of discussion is rising. There has never been anything like this—people watching how the leadership is changing.[13]

The Congress had two main tasks. It elected a new Supreme Soviet of 542 members. The Supreme Soviet was the country's new parliament. Its job was to run the country between the annual meetings of the Congress of People's Deputies. The Congress also elected, though not without dissent, a new president of the Soviet Union. This job was given far more power than in the past. To nobody's surprise, the new president, with more than 95 percent of the vote, was Mikhail Gorbachev. Just before the vote Gorbachev stood before the Congress and answered questions and criticism. He accepted them, he said, in a "comradely spirit." Then he made an emotional promise to the delegates and the nation:

> *All of us today are just learning democracy. We are only now forming a political culture. . . . I will never allow the thing that happened in our past to happen again.*[14]

Gorbachev obviously had to push hard for these political changes. One aspect of his reforms that seemed to run better on its own was *glasnost*. For three generations, the state controlled information in the Soviet Union. It told people which books they could read, which movies they could see, what kinds of art they could view, and what they should like and dislike. It controlled the news; the press and media printed and broadcast what it was told. *Glasnost* began as a small glimmer of uncensored material in 1985. It suffered a brief setback when the government tried to cover up the Chernobyl disaster during its first days. But it quickly began to flow again, becoming a steady beam during late 1986 and early 1987, and a glaring beacon after that.

Glasnost had many aspects. It was the publication of once forbidden authors like Mikhail Bulgakov and Vladimir Nabokov, whose careers dated from the early years of the Bolshevik Revolution. It was the appearance of books like Nobel Prize–winner Boris Pasternak's *Dr. Zhivago*, which had never been printed in the Soviet Union. It meant that Soviet citizens could finally read Anatoli Rybakov's *Children of the Arbat* and Vassily Grossman's *Forever Flowing*, both of which dealt boldly with Stalin's crimes. In 1989 came the stunning announcement that Alexsandr Solzhenitsyn's *Gulag Archipelago* would be published in his native land. Solzhenitsyn, a survivor of Stalin's labor camps, was forcibly exiled from the Soviet Union in 1974. Of all the current Russian critics of the Soviet system, he may be the one Soviet authorities fear and resent the most.

Glasnost let the Soviet people see films like *Repentance* in 1987, three years after it was made. This exposé of Stalin played to over 700,000 viewers in Moscow in only ten *days*, prior to being released all over the country. It was only one of over 100 banned films released between 1985 and 1988. In 1989 *Little Vera*, a new film about the frustration and hardship of Soviet working-class life, was released. The movie dealt frankly with topics like alcoholism and terrible living conditions. It also focused on youthful sexuality in a number of explicit scenes that broke all the rules Soviet censors had once strictly enforced.

Glasnost also gave the people of the Soviet Union the chance to display and view new types of art and listen to music muffled or silenced for decades. In 1987, Sergei Rachmaninoff's *Vespers,* a work with strong religious overtones, filled a Leningrad concert hall after decades of being banned. Meanwhile rock and roll, once denounced as a "crime of the people," emerged from the underground. Aquarium, the best-known Soviet rock group, was finally permitted to release an album. Without a single advertisement, 200,000 copies sold out within hours. By the middle of 1989, three million copies had been sold. Soviet rock received another enormous boost in 1988 when Paul McCartney, the legendary former Beatle, released an album called *Back in the USSR* for distribution exclusively in the Soviet Union. Officially priced at about $7, its price on the black market soared as high as $250.

Glasnost also extended to the serious matters of history. Gorbachev had referred to what he calls the "blank pages" in Soviet history. They are more than that, as the official version of Soviet history since 1917 distorts reality beyond recognition. These blank pages now began to be filled in, starting with the crimes of the Stalin era.

One problem for Gorbachev and the authorities is that the almost daily doses of shocking new material have created confusion as well as enlightenment. By 1988 the situation was so bad that history textbooks in the schools had to be withdrawn and exams for the academic year canceled. Another problem is that the process of telling the truth has no natural end. Gorbachev wants to discredit Stalin, but insists he reveres Lenin. But under *glasnost* some historians have begun to criticize Lenin as well. This disturbs the authorities because Lenin was the founder of the Bolshevik party and Soviet state. It is one thing to debunk Stalin. However, if Lenin's reputation suffers too much, Gorbachev will have a hard time explaining just what has gone right since 1917.

If *glasnost*-inspired information about the present is any guide, there is also a great deal going wrong today. Once the Soviet people were told only how well their country was doing. Now they hear about corruption, poverty, murders, drug addiction, inflation, and prostitution. They know the dreadful story about how AIDS was spread to twenty-seven children when nurses lacking access to new needles used contaminated ones. They know immediately about disasters, not only Chernobyl, but tragedies like the sinking of a cruise ship, with the loss of 398 lives, and the accidental sinking of a Soviet nuclear submarine.

Since 1985 Gorbachev has relaxed the pressure on those who openly dissent from official policies. Among those who benefited was Andrei Sakharov, the world renowned nuclear scientist and human rights advocate. He was released from years of exile in a provincial city and allowed to return to Moscow late in 1986. In 1989, he was elected to the Congress of People's Deputies.

A few bold people have even organized themselves into political groups outside the party. These organizations have taken different forms. There are a number of them in the non-Russian republics fighting for local

*Physicist and human rights advocate
Andrei Sakharov arrives in Moscow after
spending seven years of exile in Gorky.*

rights. One group with a broader perspective is the "Democratic Union," a coalition of about 100 groups organized late in 1988.

The Soviets also have eased their emigration policies. This has especially helped the Jewish community. Reflecting a long history of discrimination before and after 1917, many Soviet Jews emigrated when given the chance during the 1970s and more want to do so today. Still, even as they enjoy their new freedom, there are many who wonder if it will last. For example, in 1988 a leading Armenian dissident suddenly was stripped of his Soviet citizenship and deported. Sakharov expressed his fears on this issue, as have other dissidents. One put it this way: "I am not over-optimistic. . . . I'm very glad we have something, but no one knows how far it will go."[15]

One thing that has remained a mystery to Gorbachev and his associates is how to solve his country's economic problems. There have been a number of major reforms. Allowing factories more freedom was one. New laws permit people to go into business for themselves under certain conditions. Perhaps the most dramatic step is the new farm policy Gorbachev announced in March 1989. He wants to allow farmers to lease land themselves for fifty years. This in effect will turn them into private farmers, reversing the failed policy of collective farming.

But overhauling a gigantic economy is a massive job that, at best, will take many years to show results. In the meantime, Gorbachev must ask the Soviet people to work hard with little promise of immediate reward. They have heard this refrain before, and are not likely to respond enthusiastically to it. Even worse, the confusion associated with Gorbachev's reforms has combined with long-standing inefficiencies to produce new problems. The 1988 grain harvest was the worst in three years. By 1989, many consumer goods were in shorter supply than before 1985 and some are being rationed. The per person production of basics like grain, potatoes, and vegetables fell for several years. The budget deficit, a problem before 1985, has increased, in part because of revenues lost from lower alcohol sales, a result of one of Gorbachev's most publicized policies. When measured as a percentage of the total economy, the Soviet budget deficit is about triple that of the United States. Western observers generally agree that Gorbachev is going to have to show some real progress soon. Otherwise he can expect massive outbursts of popular discontent and an uncertain future.

A problem potentially even more serious than the economy is the nationalities question. Centuries of expansion brought many non-Russians under Russian control before 1917. The Soviet Union is really a modernized version of that empire. Almost half of its population is non-Russian. Many of those minorities do not like control from Moscow. Often they do not like each other, either. Before *glasnost, demokratisatzia,* and *perestroika,* most of these tensions were kept under control. Since 1985, however, they have burst into the open across the land.

In Latvia, Lithuania, and Estonia, in the western part of the country along the Baltic Sea (see map of the Soviet Union on pages 14–15), massive demonstrations and newly formed political groups are demanding more freedom to run their local affairs. There are even calls for independence in these republics, which were independent between 1918 and 1940, before the Soviet Union annexed them after Stalin's notorious 1939 treaty with Nazi Germany. In the south, close to Gorbachev's native Stavropol, trouble of another kind has exploded in the Caucasus. There age-old conflicts between Armenians and Azerbaijanis, Georgians and Abkhazians, and Georgians and Russians produced riots and street fighting that cost many lives and created several hundred thousand refugees. In Central Asia, Kazakh resentment against Russians continues to cause trouble, while ethnic violence in Uzbekistan has cost dozens of lives and forced the evacuation of thousands of members of the small Meskhetian minority living there.

Elsewhere the situation is quieter, but there are many rumblings. Of most concern to the Kremlin is the Ukraine. The Ukrainians are very closely related to the Russians, but many of them still resent Russian domination over their land that dates from the seventeenth century. The nationalities problem, which is growing every day, is therefore considered by many experts to be the most serious of the Soviet Union's long-term problems. As the 1980s drew to a close and the 1990s began, it was also the most worrisome immediate threat to Communist party general secretary and Soviet president Mikhail Gorbachev.

8
FROM THE EIGHTIES
TO THE NINETIES

As the waning months of 1989 signaled the passage from one decade to another, Mikhail Gorbachev could point with pride to what he had achieved as leader of his country. His *glasnost* policies had changed the Soviet cultural, artistic, and literary landscape, in many cases beyond recognition. Bold initiatives had been introduced in economic affairs. Soviet political life had been awakened after an enforced slumber of seventy years. Relations with other countries had improved dramatically, most importantly with the United States. And Mikhail Gorbachev had become the most internationally respected Soviet leader in history, and possibly the most popular head of state in the world.

Gorbachev's international standing was demonstrated again several times during 1989. In June he received a wildly enthusiastic welcome on a visit to West Germany. In December Gorbachev took a major step of reconciliation when he went to Rome and became the first Soviet leader ever to meet with the pope. That meeting was followed by a very successful summit with American president George Bush on the Mediterranean island of Malta. The two leaders spoke for many when they issued a statement announcing a new era in Soviet-American relations.

If anything could dwarf Gorbachev's successes and image, it is the enormity of the problems he still faces.

139

The historic meeting
between Gorbachev and
Pope John Paul II
marked the first
time a Kremlin
chief met with
a Roman Catholic
pontiff.

The economic crisis was underscored in July by a massive series of coal strikes. They began in Siberia and soon spread to the European part of the country. Soon more than 100,000 miners were on strike and the entire economy was threatened with paralysis. Order was restored when the government promised immediate action to improve the miserable living conditions at the mines. But although Gorbachev expressed sympathy for the miners and was able to get them back to work, their anger clearly was shared by other workers. The threat of other crippling strikes, which could complicate or derail *perestroika,* was real and continuous. Gorbachev therefore urged the new Supreme Soviet to ban strikes for fifteen months. As a sign of the times, it gave Gorbachev only part of what he wanted. Instead of a total ban, the parliament passed a law banning strikes in certain critical industries, but allowing them under certain conditions in most others.

Other problems were at least as threatening. This was especially true of the nationalities issues. The summer of 1989 witnessed more agitation in Lithuania, Latvia, and Estonia. Passions heated up in August, the fiftieth anniversary of the Stalin-Hitler treaty that paved the way for the Soviet annexation of those countries. The boiling point was reached again at the end of the year. In December, the Lithuanian legislature defied Moscow when it voted to abolish the Lithuanian Communist party's monopoly on political power. In an attempt to win public support at home, the Lithuanian Communist party declared itself separate from the Communist party of the Soviet Union. In January 1990 Gorbachev himself responded with a dramatic visit to Lithuania and a passionate personal appeal to its people to halt their pressure for independence. His visit had little visible effect on the local mood. In March Lithuania declared its independence. While it could not in reality enforce that declaration, little Lithuania became a giant symbol of

141

the Soviet Union's, and Mikhail Gorbachev's, nationalities problem.

New trouble also erupted in the Caucasus, where tension between Armenians and Azerbaijanis brought the region to the brink of civil war. For several months late in 1989 the Azerbaijanis blockaded railroad supply routes to the Armenian SSR. The new year began badly. In Azerbaijan, violence flared and over seventy people died in only a few days; many of them were Armenian victims of Azerbaijani mobs. With civilians on both sides arming themselves, Gorbachev was forced to proclaim a state of emergency and send a reinforcement of 11,000 soldiers to the region.

Meanwhile Gorbachev faced political opposition back in Moscow. Sharp differences surfaced in June at the first session of the new Supreme Soviet. Gorbachev again was criticized by people like Boris Yeltsin for going too slowly. Meanwhile Yeltsin emerged as the unofficial head of a group of deputies called the Interregional Group. It was committed to a faster pace of change. Actually Gorbachev was more concerned by the conservative forces led by Yegor Ligachev that remained entrenched at all levels of the party. The general secretary moved against the conservatives in the fall. Three of Ligachev's allies

A mourner lifts his arms in grief under a statue of Lenin during a mass funeral in the Soviet Azerbaijan capital of Baku. The funeral service was for those killed in the ethnic violence and armed resistance that ravaged the capital.

were removed from the Politburo in the fall and replaced by two reformers. This considerably strengthened Gorbachev in the Communist party's most powerful body and probably gave him a genuine workable minority there for the first time.

Gorbachev's Politburo victory still left conservatives in powerful positions in many other party bodies. There were also some ultraconservative groups of undetermined strength that operated independently. The best known of them is called Pamyat, the Russian word for memory. Pamyat advocates extreme Russian nationalism. It is anti-Western at a time when Gorbachev is trying to improve relations with the West. It is also strongly anti-Semitic at a time when he is struggling to combat a variety of traditional prejudices.

Beyond that loomed more problems for Gorbachev. During the 1980s the Soviet Union had several environmental disasters other than Chernobyl. One of the worst was in the south, where a large salt lake called the Aral Sea was drying up because the rivers flowing into the lake had too much of their water diverted for irrigation purposes. As the Aral Sea continued to shrink, huge salt beds were exposed to the air. As winds blew the salt away, it landed on and began to ruin large areas of farmland. This and other environmental problems gave rise to a number of advocacy groups concerned with such issues as nuclear power and pollution. These groups demanded solutions to these problems. Gorbachev was sympathetic to their concerns, as he has made clear a number of times. His problem was to find the resources to improve the environment while trying to do so many other things for an increasingly impatient population.

The Soviet population was not only impatient, it was also fearful and suspicious. For centuries the Russian peasant had lived in a world where few were allowed to get ahead. The emphasis was on a rough, if miserable, equality. This group mentality was reinforced after 1917 by the propaganda of a government committed to socialism. As a result, there has always been widespread resentment of any program that permits some individuals to prosper while others remain poor. One example of this was the public attitude to the new private businesses permitted by Gorbachev's reforms. While in the United States people are admired if they can successfully start a new business, in the Soviet Union private business people who make a lot of money often are accused of "robbing" their fellow citizens.

Yet Gorbachev was trying to stimulate individual initiative. He insisted and believed that any Soviet individual initiative would remain within the framework of socialism, but many working people in the Soviet Union were not convinced that he was telling the truth. They also worried that Gorbachev's emphasis on efficiency would lead to many people losing their jobs. In short, Gorbachev will have to work hard to retain the confidence of millions of ordinary Soviet citizens.

In foreign affairs, Gorbachev was having at least as many problems with Communist countries as with capitalist ones. The Soviet Union had controlled Eastern Europe since the end of World War II, when Communist regimes were established there under the gun of the Red Army. This was the Soviet Union's greatest prize from that costly war, and every Soviet leader since then expressed his determination to maintain his country's influence in the region. Both Khrushchev in the 1950s and Brezhnev in the 1960s used military force to prevent Eastern European Communist regimes from collapsing. Shortly after his election as general secretary, Gorbachev had announced his determination to preserve close Soviet ties with Eastern Europe. From the beginning, however, many observers wondered how he could make meaningful reforms at home without losing control of Eastern Europe, where most of the local Communist regimes had failed miserably and had very little public support.

During the summer and fall of 1989 the answer to that question came with stunning suddenness. Unable to count on Soviet military support because of Gorbachev's "new thinking," and undermined as their people learned about genuine reform in Russia, Communist regimes of Eastern Europe began to cave in. The process began in Poland. There the thoroughly unpopular and increasingly desperate government agreed to free elections in June in an attempt to win public support. The Communists were humiliated as they were totally defeated in Poland's first free election since World War II. In August Poland's first non-Communist government in over forty years took office. Next on the list was Hungary. Early in October the Hungarian Communist party had actually voted to disband itself and reorganize as the Socialist party. Hungary itself was declared a multiparty democracy, ending four decades as a Communist dictatorship, and free elections were scheduled for 1990. By the end of October increasing pressure forced the hard-line party leadership in Bulgaria to resign. The new leaders, while still Communists, soon promised what they called "free and democratic elections" within a year.

The most dramatic events took place in East Germany, supposedly the most successful Communist state in Eastern Europe. During the summer of 1989, as East Germany's neighbors started to open up their borders with Western Europe, tens of thousands of East Germans began to flee to the West. At home hundreds of thousands of demonstrators took to the streets. By October the turmoil brought down the old leadership. The new leaders, still Communists, tried to stem the human tide rushing to the West by doing what until the moment it happened was unthinkable. On November 9, 1989, the notorious Berlin Wall was opened to unre-

146

stricted travel to the West. For over a quarter century the Berlin Wall had stood as the grim symbol of the division of Europe. What had been the scene of desperate escape attempts—some successful, many futile and fatal—now became a place of celebration. As thousands of people crossed back and forth, others danced atop its concrete blocks or struck the hated wall with chisels and sledgehammers. By December additional reforms, further ousters of party leaders, and the promise of elections the following spring signaled the approaching end of Communist power in East Germany.

The upheaval in East Germany raised at least one troubling issue, even for people in the West. Should the two Germanies now be allowed to reunite? This would create the most powerful nation in Europe west of the Soviet Union. If a united Germany worried Gorbachev and his colleagues in the Kremlin, at least they knew they were not alone. Such a prospect also was of great concern to people throughout the world who remembered the horrors of World War II.

The day after the Berlin Wall was opened, Todor Zhivkov resigned after thirty-five years as the undisputed strongman in Bulgaria and the process of reform began there. Two weeks later pressure from all sides forced the hard-line Czechoslovakian party leadership to resign. By the end of December, Czechoslovakia had its first non-Communist government since 1948, headed by a playwright named Vaclav Havel. Change also finally came to Romania, but unlike elsewhere in Eastern Europe, only after tragic violence. In mid-December Communist dictator Nicolae Ceausescu's secret police forces massacred many pro-democracy demonstrators. Still the demonstrations continued. When the Romanian army refused orders to shoot the people it was supposed to protect and joined them instead, protest became revolution. Several days of bloody fighting followed, during which Ceausescu and his wife Elena were captured while trying to flee, and executed. A quickly formed "National Salvation Front" took power and promised a multiparty political system and free elections.

Meanwhile, Gorbachev did nothing to stop or slow the continental Communist collapse. In effect, he seemed to have calculated that Soviet security depended on good relations with the West and on diverting his country's resources from military to civilian use. These priorities made it impossible to save Eastern Europe's unpopular and unreliable Communist regimes. *Perestroika* in the Soviet Union had produced political restructuring in Eastern Europe.

To the east of the Soviet Union was another Communist problem: the People's Republic of China. Gorbachev became the first Soviet leader to visit China in thirty years when he went to Beijing in the spring of 1989. Although the visit was relatively successful, Gorbachev still had a lot of fence-mending to do to overcome three decades of hostility. At the same time, he had to continue to improve relations with the capitalist world, especially the United States. As the 1990s dawned, the will to build on the progress already made seemed to exist on both sides. It remained to be seen if the way would be found to do so.

Back in Moscow, early 1990 witnessed Gorbachev's most dramatic political step yet. Since 1917, the Communist party had claimed the right to a monopoly of political power in the Soviet Union. In February, under pressure from events in Eastern Europe, the party heeded Gorbachev's urging and officially gave up that claim. While the Communist party still controlled the Soviet Union, this concession increased the prospects for further democratization of Soviet society. At the same time, Gorbachev solidified his own power. He convinced the party and then the parliament to create a new presidency, the second time this had been done in less than a year. The new office was given greatly expanded powers, including the right to impose economic regulations by decree. It also would be filled by direct election by the Soviet people, although Gorbachev insisted that the first president should be chosen by the Congress of People's Deputies because the country was in too much turmoil for a presidential campaign. To nobody's surprise, the Congress of People's Deputies then chose Mikhail Gorbachev to be the Soviet Union's new president.

On March 11, 1990, Mikhail Gorbachev marked his fifth anniversary in power. The pyramid diagram below

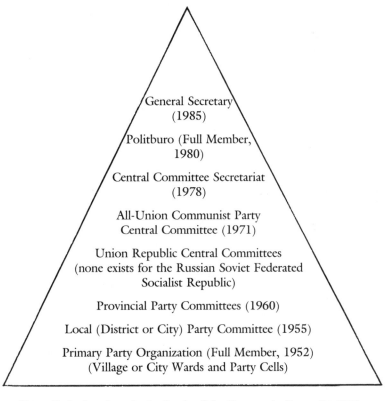

Years Gorbachev Ascends the Ranks of the Communist Party. In 1990, as President of the Soviet Union, he was building a power base outside the Communist Party.

summarizes his rapid ascent through the Soviet political hierarchy. In that time he has managed to bring a new vitality to almost every aspect of Soviet life. Yet old fears and problems—the products not only of seventy years of Communist rule but of centuries of tsarist rule—lie just below the surface. He has done much to improve the Soviet Union's relations with other nations. In particular, a successful Washington summit meeting with American president George Bush in June 1990 produced important arms control agreements. But old suspicions and the pain of past injuries have not gone away. During the early 1990s Gorbachev's popularity abroad contrasted sharply with his falling stature at home, especially as the Soviet economy continued to deteriorate.

Mikhail Gorbachev in many ways was the most important political development of the 1980s. One American news organization underscored this by naming him the "Man of the Decade" in 1989. The question for the future is whether he can continue to develop the promise of the 1980s into the successes of the 1990s. Upon that will depend not just the future of one man, but a significant part of the future of a great country and the world in which it must live.

Soviet president Mikhail Gorbachev delivers his acceptance speech after the newly formed Congress of People's Deputies elected him head of state.

SOURCE NOTES

Chapter One

1. Victor Kravchenko, *I Chose Justice* (New York: Charles Scribner's Sons, 1950), pp. 99–100.
2. cited in Moshe Lewin, *Russian Peasants and Soviet Power: A Study of Collectivization,* trans. Irene Nove (New York: Norton, 1975), p. 596.
3. Mikhail Gorbachev, *Perestroika: New Thinking for Our Country and the World,* new, updated ed. (New York: Harper and Row, 1987), pp. 26–27.
4. cited in Roy Medvedev, *Let History Judge,* trans. Colleen Taylor, ed. David Joravsky and Georges Haupt (New York: Vintage Books, 1971), p. 95.
5. Gorbachev, *Perestroika,* p. 27.
6. "The MacNeil Lehrer News Hour," a PBS television news program, August 30, 1989.

Chapter Two

1. Introduction to Mikhail Gorbachev, *A Time for Peace* (New York: Richardson and Steirman, 1985), p. 9.
2. *The Wall Street Journal,* March 12, 1985.
3. cited in Dusko Doder, *Shadows and Whispers: Power Politics Inside the Kremlin from Brezhnev to Gorbachev* (New York: Random House, 1986), p. 284.
4. cited in Zhores A. Medvedev, *Gorbachev* (New York and London: Norton, 1986), p. 39.
5. cited in *The Wall Street Journal,* March 12, 1985.
6. Donald Morrison, ed., *Mikhail S. Gorbachev: An Intimate Biography* (New York: *Time,* 1988), p. 71.

7. Zdenek Mlynar, "Il mio compagno di studi Mikhail Gorbachev," *L'Unita,* April 9, 1985.
8. cited in Morrison, p. 64.

Chapter Three
1. cited in Martin Walker, *The Waking Giant: Gorbachev's Russia* (New York: Pantheon, 1986), p. 6.
2. cited in *Morrison,* p. 83.
3. Nikita S. Khrushchev, *The Crimes of the Stalin Era* (New York: *The New Leader,* 1962), pp. 25–27.
4. Yevgeny Yevtushenko, "The Heirs of Stalin," *The Poetry of Yevgeny Yevtushenko* (New York: October House, 1965), pp. 41–42.
5. "Mikhail Gorbachyov," *Soviet Weekly,* March 16, 1985.
6. Mikhail Gorbachev, *At the Summit: Speeches and Interviews, February 1987–July 1988* (New York: Richardson, Steirman, & Black, 1988), p. 93.
7. Z. Medvedev, *Gorbachev,* p. 64.
8. Mikhail Gorbachev, *M. S. Gorbachev: Speeches and Writings,* vol 2. (Oxford: Pergamon Press, 1987) p. 203.

Chapter Four
1. cited in Morrison, p. 88.
2. cited in Walker, p. 16.
3. *Pravda,* July 16, 1977.
4. *Izvestiya,* September 29, 1983.
5. cited in Z. Medvedev, *Gorbachev,* p. 86.
6. *Pravda,* July 20, 1978.

Chapter Five
1. Zhores Medvedev, *Soviet Agriculture* (New York and London: Norton, 1987), pp. 408–409.
2. cited in Morrison, pp. 123–124.
3. cited in Thomas G. Butson, *Gorbachev: A Biography* (New York: Stein and Day, 1985), p. 70.
4. "The Novosibirsk Report," in Robert V. Daniels, ed., *A Documentary History of Communism,* vol. I, updated, revised ed. (Hanover and London: University Press of New England, 1988), p. 246.
5. cited in Christian Schmidt-Hauer, *Gorbachev: The Path to Power* (London: I. B. Tauris, 1986), p. 192.

6. *Pravda,* June 28, 1984.
7. *Newsweek,* March 25, 1985.
8. cited in Dev Muraka, *Gorbachev: The Limits of Power* (London: Hutchinson, 1988), p. 127.
9. cited in Dodor, *Shadows and Whispers,* p. 267.

Chapter Six
1. Mikhail Gorbachev, *M. S. Gorbachev: Speeches and Writings,* p. 205.
2. ibid., p. 207.
3. cited in Morrison, p. 210.
4. Walker, pp. 178–179.
5. *The New York Times,* May 27, 1989.
6. Gorbachev, *Perestroika,* p. 1.
7. ibid., p. 61.
8. ibid., p. 212.
9. Schmidt-Hauer, p. 162.
10. Mikhail Gorbachev, *Towards a Better World* (New York: Richardson and Steirman, 1987), p. 109.
11. cited in Morrison, p. 146.
12. Gorbachev, *Perestroika,* p. 222.
13. ibid., p. 221.

Chapter Seven
1. cited in Michael Mandelbaum and Strobe Talbot, *Reagan and Gorbachev* (New York: Vintage Books, 1987), p. 173.
2. Gorbachev, *Towards a Better World,* pp. 32, 35.
3. *Time,* July 27, 1987.
4. cited in *Mikhail S. Gorbachev,* pp. 216–217.
5. Gorbachev, *At the Summit,* p. 96.
6. ibid., p. 167.
7. *The New York Times,* February 16, 1988.
8. *The New York Times,* December 8, 1988.
9. ibid.
10. *The New York Times,* July 2, 1988.
11. *The Boston Globe,* May 30, 1989.
12. *The New York Times,* April 27, 1989.
13. *The New York Times,* June 1, 1989.
14. *The New York Times,* May 31, 1989.
15. *The Boston Globe,* May 11, 1989.

FURTHER READING

Aganbegyan, Abel, ed. *Perestroika 1989*. New York: Charles Scribner's Sons, 1988.

Daniels, Robert V. *Is Russia Reformable?* Boulder, Colo., and London: Westview Press, 1988.

Davies, R. W. *Soviet History in the Gorbachev Revolution*. Bloomington and Indianapolis: Indiana University Press, 1989.

Desai, Padma. *Perestroika in Perspective*. Princeton, N.J.: Princeton University Press, 1989.

Eklof, Ben. *Soviet Briefing*. Boulder, Colo., and London: Westview Press, 1989.

Goldman, Marshall L. *Gorbachev's Challenge: Economic Reform in the Age of High Technology*. New York and London: Norton, 1987.

Hough, Jerry. *Russia and the West: Gorbachev and the Politics of Reform*. New York: Simon and Schuster, 1988.

Kerblay, Basile. *Gorbachev's Russia*. New York: Pantheon, 1989.

Kort, Michael. *The Soviet Colossus: A History of the USSR*, 2d ed. Boston and London: Unwin Hyman, 1990.

Lewin, Moshe. *The Gorbachev Phenomenon*. Berkeley and Los Angeles: University of California Press, 1989.

Oberg, James E. *Uncovering Soviet Disasters: Exploring the Limits of Glasnost*. New York: Random House, 1988.

Rywkin, Michael. *Soviet Society Today*. New York: M. E. Sharpe, 1989.

Tarasulo, Isaac J., ed. *Gorbachev and Glasnost: Viewpoints from the Soviet Press*. Wilmington, Del.: Scholarly Resources, 1989.

Taubman, William, and Jane Taubman. *Moscow Spring*. New York: Summit Books, 1989.

INDEX